The Audacity of Prayer

A Fresh Translation
of the Book of Psalms

(English Edition)

Translated by John Cunyus

The Audacity of Prayer
A Fresh Translation of the Book of Psalms
(English Edition)

Translated by John Cunyus
with a foreword by Reverend Joseph Harker.

Contributors include
Myles Hall
Reverend Tony Salisbury

ISBN # 978-0-9644609-9-7

©2009, John G. Cunyus
All Rights to the English Translation and Commentary Reserved.
All Rights to Cover art Reserved.
www.JohnCunyus.com.

Latin text from "The Latin Vulgate." *Biblia Sacra Iuxta Vulgatam Versionem*,
Fourth Revised Edition, edited by Roger Gryson,
© 1994 Deutsche Bibelgesellschaft, Stuttgart. Used by permission.

Searchlight Press
Who are you looking for?
Publishers of thoughtful Christian books since 1994.
PO Box 482
Glen Rose, Texas 76042
888.896.6081
info@Searchlight-Press.com
www.Searchlight-Press.com
www.JohnCunyus.com

To the Reverend Doctor Robert Gartman,
encourager, pastor, and friend.

Table of Contents

Foreword   Pg. 5
   by Joseph Harker

About the Project   Pg. 7

Introduction to the Book of Psalms   Pg. 9

How to Pray the Psalms   Pg. 13

The Book of Psalms   Pg. 15

Foreword

Near the opening of the previous century, the essayist Marcel Proust famously pronounced that "The voyage of discovery consists not seeking new landscapes, but in having new eyes." Now, as our new century continues to unfold, adventurers who seek the truth within the pages of the Holy Bible are acquiring new eyes through which to reconnoiter a landscape that was already ancient when Saint Jerome first popularized it in Latin some sixteen centuries ago.

Rev. Cunyus' translation of Psalms is thus new and age-old in a single stroke. But just how old is it? Is it freshly minted, since his word-choices in his new English translation represent a "vernacular" for the 21st century? Or perhaps his work is really 1600 years old, since it consists partly of Jerome's masterful translation into the "vulgar" Latin of the later Roman Imperium. Then again, the words of the Psalmist stretch back to the original Israelite worship of God before the Ark of the Covenant. To be honest, John's work stretches back to the very origin of the human race, in its attempt to put the things of God into "modern" human language. In all those millennia, God hasn't changed; neither has human nature, for that matter. Only the words change, while the Psalm remains the same.

And therein likes the power of Jerome's text in the hands of the modern (or post-modern) reader; these words from Psalms in Latin have shaped the poetry, religion, and world-view of the West. For those of us in need of a translation to understand Jerome's Latin text, Rev. Cunyus' gift has been to show us the pervasive similarity between age-old Latin and the English of our own time. Although my Latin was never very good, even I am struck by the cognates which my own faltering eye can discern. To limit myself to a single example, the Latin phrase *de profundis*, that begins Vulgate Psalm 129 for instance, conjures up new images "out of the depths" of my own soul; reminding me of just how profound the Bible is, in any language.

New eyes indeed.

Reverend Joseph Harker
Wylie, Texas
January 28, 2009

About the Project

In 2008, John Cunyus and Searchlight Press began the process of translating the Latin Old Testament into contemporary English.

The first books translated in the series were Job, Proverbs, Ecclesiastes, and the Song of Solomon. These were published by Searchlight Press as The Way of Wisdom: Job, Proverbs, Ecclesiastes, Song of Solomon, in both an English and a Latin-English edition.

The next book translated was Psalms, using Jerome's Septuagint translation. This volume now appears as English and Latin-English versions of The Audacity of Prayer: A Fresh Translation of the Book of Psalms.

At present, John is translating the Minor Prophets.

Why On Earth Would Anyone Want To Do that?

That was the question from a longtime Episcopal rector, on hearing about this Latin Bible translation project. It's a good question. Why Latin, rather than Hebrew? Why a new translation, when there are already others out there?

Here are a few answers in a nutshell:

1. Latin is a different textual tradition. As we struggle to realize all the time, "different" does not mean "worse," "wrong," or "defective." The Latin text is ancient, voluminously attested, and critically studied, as are the others.

It is something of a "road less traveled" now, given the almost exclusive interest in Hebrew and Greek among contemporary scholars. In addition to the translator's profound respect for Patristic Christianity, we also like to take "roads less traveled." You see the unexpected more readily on them.

2. The Latin text makes the Christological aspects of the Old Testament clearer. The Latin text itself is the root of

much Western theology and church practice. As a historical document alone, it warrants study. When the Latin text was constructed, scholars like Jerome still had access to many texts and traditions that were lost in the aftermath of Rome's fall, the Muslim conquests, the Crusades, and other subsequent upheavals.

3. The oldest extant Latin Bible, containing all the books we know in our Bibles today (plus a few extras) predates the oldest Masoretic (Hebrew) text by three centuries. *Codex Amiatinus*, produced in Northumbria, England, in the 7th Century CE, is now in a library in Florence, Italy.

4. New translations matter because our language changes. Since Latin is such a terse language, it offers us the opportunity to compress English into something similar. As the *Tao Te Ching* says, "More words count less." Jerome certainly understood that.

None of these reasons takes anything away at all from other textual traditions. Working from the Latin can make something very old seem new, which interests many. And, of course, the Bible remains the Bible, whatever the language.

The most important reason is this: 5. It's a way of "glorifying the One who speaks through the words of scripture." Whether anyone else ever gets anything out of this project or not, we hope that's what this project does.

Introduction to The Book of Psalms

This collection of religious poems is known in Judaism as "The Book of Praises." Among Christians, it is called "The Book of Psalms." The word "psalm" is a Greek word meaning a song sung to musical accompaniment. The Book of Psalms is often referred to as the Psalter.

According to Charles Ryrie, the Book of Psalms is itself divided into five sub-books, the length of each more or less determined by the length of ancient scrolls. Each of the five books within the Book of Psalms would fit on one scroll, just as each of the five books of the Law would.[1]

Book I: Psalms 1-41.
Book II: Psalms 42-72.
Book III: Psalms 73-89.
Book IV: Psalms 90-106.
Book V: Psalms 107-150.

The numbering of the Psalms in the Vulgate is slightly different from Dr. Ryrie's divisions above. The Vulgate Psalter combines Psalms 9 and 10 from standard English translations. Psalm 147, in turn, is divided in the Vulgate into two separate Psalms. Thus, many English favorites, such as Psalm 23, are numbered differently in the Latin. I have added the standard English numbering to the beginnings of each of the Psalms effected by this difference, for the reader's convenience.

The work, originally written in Hebrew, was translated into Greek in the 3rd Century before Christ.[2] In the 3rd Century of the Common Era, the great Christian scholar Origen created *The Hexapla*, a multi-columned version of what we know of as The Old Testament, as a way of correcting the errors that had crept into the text at the hands of copyists

---

[1] *The Ryrie Study Bible: New International Version*, Charles Ryrie, editor. Moody Press, Chicago, 1986, pg. 723.

[2] *The New Encyclopaedia Britannica*, Volume 12, Micropaedia, Encyclopedia Britannica, Chicago, 1998, pg. 438

through the centuries.[3]

Jerome, who translated the Old Testament into Latin between 383 and 405 CE, used Origen's *Hexapla* in creating his translations. Jerome's text, then, represents the high-water mark of classical, Latin-based, biblical scholarship. It became the standard Bible of the Western church for several hundred years.[4]

There are two versions of the Psalter associated with Jerome's translations. In the first version, he revised and corrected an existing *Vetus Latina*, or "Old Latin," translation of the Septuagint, the earlier Greek translation, which had become the Bible of the Christian church. Not totally satisfied, he decided to craft another translation from the Hebrew itself.[5] This decision led Jerome, already a middle-aged man, to study Hebrew at the feet of Jewish rabbis, in order to pass Hebrew scripture on more faithfully to Christian readers.

Both versions of the Psalms survived, each one playing the prominent role in various different locations. In Gaul, present-day France, Jerome's Septuagint translation of the Psalms was used most commonly in the Old Testament. Alcuin, an English scholar called to Charlemagne's court, standardized the so-called Gallican Psalter for the Church at large.[6] It became the definitive Vulgate Psalter thereafter, though the other translation also survived.[7]

---

[3] The New Encyclopaedia Britannica, Volume 8, Micropedia, Encyclopaedia Britannica, Chicago, 1988, pgs 997-999

[4] See http://www.newadvent.org/cathen/07316a.htm.

[5] See http://www.newadvent.org/cathen/05286a.htm.

[6] See http://www.newadvent.org/cathen/01276a.htm.

[7] Biblia Sacra Iuxta Vulgatam Versionem, Fourth Revised Edition. Roger Gryson, editor, Deutsche Bibelgesellschaft, Stuttgart, 1994, pgs xxx-xxxi. Hereafter cited as Vulgate.

Because the Gallican Psalter was based on the Septuagint, it more accurately reflects the Book of Psalms as the first generation of Hellenistic Christianity would have known it. The Hebrew-based Psalter would have been unknown to non-Jewish Christians of the early centuries. For such Christians, the Bible existed in Greek, rather than Hebrew.

Some ask, why translate a translation? What advantage is there in studying the Latin, when the original language, Hebrew, is still available?

The answer lies in the historical nature of the Bible. It exists in its original languages, certainly. Yet it also existed profoundly in Greek, Latin, and many other languages as well.

To understand historical persons and events more clearly, it helps to understand scripture as they did. Most of Jesus' contemporaries and followers knew the Bible in Greek, rather than in Hebrew. Later, when Rome's empire divided and Western Europe was increasingly cut off from the mainstream of ancient civilizations, the Bible existed in Latin.

An illustration may help. Though the book of Psalms had existed for centuries in Hebrew, it existed in Hellenistic culture from the 3rd Century B.C.E., as the Septuagint, the Bible of most of the early Christian Church.

The Greek word "Christ" translates the Hebrew *Masiach*, meaning "anointed one," or "king." Thus, the Septuagint Psalter, rendered by Jerome into the Latin Gallican Psalter, is filled with Christological references.

Reading the Septuagint or Jerome's translation of it, one sees immediately how early Christian preachers could speak about Christ using the Psalter as a source.

Modern English translators for many centuries have taken pains not to use the Greek word "Christ" in the Psalter. "Christ" has taken on too specifically Christian a meaning, obviously, to render it a fair translation of the Hebrew original.

Nevertheless, "Christ" was the word used, both in Greek-speaking synagogues and early Christian *ecclesias*. They literally could not avoid talking about "Christ" if they talked about the Psalter at all.

Such a sense of the Psalms as an intensely Christological book has vanished, largely, from contemporary thought.

Yet the Greek and Latin texts use the word Christ throughout. Perhaps reading their version of the Psalms will give more profound insight into who Christ is, at least as the original core of Greek and Latin speakers understood Him.

> John Cunyus
> Dallas, Texas
> January 1, 2009

How to Pray the Psalms

Out loud. At the top of my voice. In a remote location.

My most memorable time praying the psalms was on a camping trip in the Apache Kid National Wilderness. I arrived early, and knew I would be the only person around for hours. I climbed up onto the top of a big rock and prayed psalms out loud, at the top of my voice.
Myles Hall
Cloudcroft, New Mexico
February 3, 2009

Prayer is sleeping, waking, walking, jumping, running, dancing, imagining, listening with God. The Book of Psalms is full of this type of prayer. Psalms are to be read before going to sleep in order to relax the soul. There are psalms to pray at the waking of the day for strength. Psalms make us want to jump and dance at the delight of God. Psalms meet our needs in how we either walk or run through the activities of daily living. Psalms assist us in how to imagine the powerful Spirit of God functioning in our lives. The Psalms open us up to listening to God in holy silence. The Book of Psalms is not only words but a constellation of experiences and emotions that move us to prayer.
Rev. Tony L. Salisbury
Abilene, Texas
February 4, 2009

Prayer is any conscious act which makes us aware of God. Speaking aloud can be prayer, just as inner conversation can be prayer. Reading the psalms is, in itself, a form of prayer. Being conscious of it as such deepens its impact.

Here are some further steps you can take. Read a passage through, reverently. Reread it several times, pausing to focus on individual parts of it that move you. Jot down notes as you go. When you finish, write a summary prayer to use again later on.
John Cunyus
Dallas, Texas
February 13, 2009

The Book of Psalms

Book One

Psalm 1:1
A man is blessed
who has not gone out
following *a* lawless counsel,
or stood up following
a sinners' way,
or sat in *the* pestilent's seat.[8]
1:2 But his will *remains*
in *the* Lord's Law,
and he will meditate
in His Law day and night.
1:3 He will be like *a* tree
which is planted
by *a* stream of water,
which will give its fruit
in its season,
and its leaf will not fall away.
In all – whatever he will do –
he will prosper.
1:4 *It is* not so
with *the* lawless!
It is not so!
But *they are* like dust,
which *the* wind blows away
from earth's face.
1:5 Therefore *the* lawless
will not rise up in judgment,
nor sinners in *the* fair ones'
counsel,
1:6 because *the* Lord
has known *the* fair ones' way.
Yet *the* lawless way
will perish.

---

[8] Use of italic case in the English translation indicates a word added in the translation that is not in the original. The English verb "is" often must be added to make grammatical sense of the Latin. Latin, like Hebrew and Greek before it, often phrased sentences without a verb, where a simple "to be" form is needed in English. Latin, unlike Greek and Hebrew, has neither definite nor indefinite articles (a, an, the). Where these are found in the translations, they are always words that have been added to make better sense of the translation.

Psalm 2:1 *A* psalm of David.

Why have nations raged
and peoples meditated
foolishness?
2:2 *The* land's kings
stood together
and princes gathered as one –
against *the* Lord
and against His Christ.[9]
2:3 "Let us break their chains
and throw their yoke
off of us!"
2:4 One who
lives in *the* skies
will laugh at them.
The Lord will mock them.
2:5 Then, He will speak
to them in His anger.
He will disturb them
in His fury.

2:6 But I am placed
as king by Him over Sion[10],
His holy mountain,
proclaiming His precept.

2:7 *The* Lord said to me,
"You are my son.
Today I bore you."[11]
2:8 Ask of me
and I will give you
nations *as* your inheritance,
and *the* land's ends
as your possession.
2:9 You will rule them
with *an* iron rod.
You will smash them
like *a* potter's vase.

2:10 And now,
kings, understand!
You who judge *the* land,
learn!
2:11 Serve *the* Lord in fear,
and exult in Him in trembling!
2:12 Take hold of discipline,
so that *the* Lord
does not get angry,
and you perish
from fairness's way
2:13 when His anger
boils over quickly!
All those who trust in Him
are blessed.

---

[9] The Greek word Christ means "anointed." It translates the Hebrew מָשִׁיחַ, designation in scripture for God's anointed King. Jerome, following the Septuagint, transliterates the Greek word Christ directly, rather than translating into Latin.

[10] Sion is the hill at the center of Jerusalem, on which David's city was built.

---

[11] The use of the first person pronoun, *Ego*, stresses that God is the One who has given him birth.

Psalm 3:1 *A* psalm of David, when he fled from *the* face of Absalom, his son.[12]

3:2 Lord,
how they are multiplied
who afflict me!
Many have risen up
against me.
3:3 Many are
saying to my soul,
"There is no security for him
in his God."
3:4 But You, Lord,
are my helper,
my glory, lifting up my head.
3:5 I cried out to *the* Lord
by my voice.
He heard me
from His holy mountain.

3:6 I slept
and was made sleepy.
I got up again,
because *the* Lord
will sustain me.

3:7 I will not fear
thousands of people
surrounding me.
Rise up, Lord!
Make me secure, my God!

3:8 For You struck all those
opposing me without cause.
You have broken
sinners' teeth.
3:9 Security is from *the* Lord.
His blessing *is* over
His people.

---

[12] For the story of Absalom's rebellion against David, see 2 Samuel 15.

Psalm 4:1 To *the* end,
in songs.
A psalm of David.

4:2 When I called,
my fairness's God heard me.
Through struggle
He broadened me.
Have mercy on me,
and hear my prayer!
4:3 Men's children, how long
will you have a heavy heart?
Why do you love vanity,
and seek lies?
4:4 You will know
that *the* Lord has made
His holy *One* wondrous.
The Lord will hear me
when I call out to Him.

4:5 Be angry but do not sin!
For what you say
on your beds in your hearts,
be repentant!
4:6 Sacrifice offerings
of fairness,
and hope in *the* Lord!

Many are saying,
"Who will show us good?"
4:7 Your face's light
is *a* sign over us.
Lord, you have given joy
in my heart,
4:8 from *the* fruit of *the* grain
and wine and oil.
They are multiplied.

4:9 I will sleep in peace
in this itself,
and find comfort,
4:10 because you, Lord,
made me remarkably in hope.

Psalm 5:1 To *the* end,
for her who follows
an inheritance.
A psalm of David.

5:2 Hear my words
with your ears, Lord!
Understand my cry!
5:3 Listen to
my prayers' voice,
my King and my God,
5:4 for I will pray to You!
Lord, You will hear
my voice early.
5:5 I will stand
before You early.
And I will see that You are
not *a* god who wills treachery,
5:6 nor will *the* malignant
live beside You,
nor will *the* unfair endure
before Your eyes.
5:7 You hated all
who work treachery.
You will destroy all
who speak *a* lie.
The Lord will detest
bloody and deceitful men.

5:8 But I will enter
into Your house
by Your mercies' multitude.
I will worship toward
Your holy temple,
in Your fear.
5:9 Lord, lead me
in Your fairness,
because of my enemies!
Guide my outlook
in Your way,
5:10 because truth isn't
in their mouth!
Their heart is
without purpose.
5:11 Their throat
is *an* open grave.
They acted deceitfully
by their tongues.
Judge them, God!
May they fall
by their *own* ideas,
according to *the* multitudes
of their lawlessness.
Drive them out because
they provoked You, Lord!

5:12 Yet may all
who hope in You
be joyful in eternity.
May they exult.
You will live in them,
and they will be glorified
in You –
all who delight in Your name.
5:13 For You will bless
by fairness, Lord,
that by good will's shield
You have crowned us.

Psalm 6:1 To *the* end,
of songs, by eighths.
A psalm of David.

6:2 Lord, do not
dispute me in Your fury,
or correct me in Your anger!
6:3 Have mercy on me, Lord,
because I am weak!
Heal me, Lord,
because my bones
are disquieted,
6:4 and my soul
is greatly troubled!

And You, Lord, how long?
6:5 Turn, Lord!
Rescue my soul!
Make me secure,
because of Your mercy,
6:6 because *there* is no one
in death who can
remember You!
Who will confess to You
in *the* inferno?

6:7 I have worked hard
in my groaning.
I will wash my bed
with my tears
through every night.
I will water my blanket.
6:8 My eye
is disturbed by fury.
I have grown old
among all my enemies.

6:9 Go away from me,
all who work betrayal,
because *the* Lord has heard
my weeping's voice!
6:10 *The* Lord has heard
my supplication.
The Lord received my prayer.
6:11 May all my enemies
be ashamed
and greatly disturbed.
May they be turned back
and be ashamed quickly

Psalm 7:1 *A* psalm of David,
which he sang to *the* Lord,
for Chusi's[13] words, Jemini's[14]
son.

7:2 Lord, my God,
I have hoped in You.
Make me secure
from all those persecuting me!
Free me,
7:3 so he does not carry away
my soul like *a* lion,
while *there* is no one
who will buy *me* back
or make me secure!

7:4 Lord, my God,
if I have done that –
if treachery is in my hands,
7:5 if I repaid harm
to those paying me harms,
let me fall deservedly
before my enemies,
worthless.
7:6 May *an* enemy
avenge my soul,
seize and trample my life
in *the* land,
and lead my fame into ashes.

7:7 Rise up, Lord!
Lift *Yourself* up
in Your anger
in my enemies' borders!
Rise up, Lord my God,
in *the* precept
which You commanded!

7:8 *The* peoples' assembly
will surround You,
and return on high
because of this.

7:9 *The* Lord judges peoples.
Judge me, Lord,
according to my fairness,
and according to
my innocence over me!
7:10 May sinners' worthless
ways be consumed!
Yet You will guide *the* fair.
God *is* scrutinizing hearts
and guts.[15]
7:11 Fairness *is* my help
from God,
who makes *the* honest
in heart secure.

7:12 God *is a* just judge,
strong and patient.
Will He be angered
every day?

---

[13] Chusi is mentioned in two other places in scripture: Jeremiah 36:14 and Zephaniah 1:1.

[14] Jemini is first mentioned in scripture at Judges 3:15.

[15] Compare to RSV: "thou who triest the minds and hearts."

7:13 Unless you are
converted,
His sword will resound.
He will bend His bow
and prepare it.
7:14 Death's vessels
are prepared in it.
He made His arrows burn.

7:15 Look, he birthed
unfairness,
conceived pain,
and brought forth betrayal.
7:16 He opened *a* pit
and dug it out.
Yet he will fall
into *the* hole he made.
7:17 His pain will turn back
on his *own* head,
His treachery will come down
on his own head.

7:18 I will confess *the* Lord,
according to His fairness,
and will sing *the* name
of *the* Lord most high.

Psalm 8:1 To *the* end,
for *the* winepresses.
A psalm of David.

8:2 Lord, our Lord,
how wonderful Your name is
in all *the* land,
because Your magnificence
is raised up above *the* skies!
8:3 From infants' mouth
and nursing children,
You have perfected praise,
because of Your enemies –
that You may destroy
enemy and avenger.
8:4 For when I see
Your skies,
Your fingers' works –
moon and stars
which You established,
8:5 what is man,
that You are mindful of him,
or man's child,
that you visit him?

8:6 You made him
little less than angels.[16]
You crowned him
with glory and honor.
8:7 You appointed him
over Your hands' works.
8:8 You subjected all things

---

[16] *Psalmi Iuxta Hebraicum* reads "*a Deo*." "You made him little less than God."

beneath his feet –
sheep and oxen all together,
and field's flocks,
8:9 sky's birds and sea's fish,
who pass along
the sea's paths.

8:10 Lord, our Lord,
how wonderful Your name is
in all *the* land!

Psalm 9:1 To *the* end
for *the* son's hidden *ones*,
a psalm of David.

9:2 I will confess to You,
Lord, with all my heart.
I will tell all Your wonders.
9:3 I will be joyful
and exult in You.
I will sing Your name,
Most High,
9:4 in turning
my enemy back.

They will grow ill
and die before Your face,
9:5 because You brought
about my judgment
and my cause.
You sat on Your throne –
You who judge fairness.
9:6 You rebuked nations,
and *the* lawless has perished.
You destroyed their name
in eternity,
and in *the* age of ages.
9:7 *The* enemies' spears
have failed in *the* end,
You destroyed cities.
Their memory perished
with *a* sound.
9:8 *The* Lord
endures to eternity.
He prepared His throne
in judgment.
9:9 He will judge

the land's circle in equity.
He will judge peoples
in fairness.

9:10 *The* Lord has become
the poor's refuge,
a helper at *the* right times
in trouble.
9:11 Let those who
know Your name
hope in You,
because You, Lord,
have not abandoned
those seeking you.

9:12 Sing psalms to *the* Lord,
who lives on Sion!
Tell His interests
among *the* nations!
9:13 For *the one* requiring
their blood is remembered.
The poor one's cry
is not forgotten.

9:14 Have mercy
on me, Lord!
See my humiliation
from my enemies!
9:15 You lift me up
from death's gates,
so I may tell all Your praises
in Sion's daughter's gates.

9:16 I will exult
in Your security.
The nations are fixed
in *the* destruction
which they made.
Their foot is caught
in *the* trap which they hid.

9:17 *The* Lord will be known,
working judgment.
The sinner is caught
by his hands' works.

9:18 May sinners
be turned to *the* inferno,
all nations that forget God!
9:19 Because *the* poor's
patience
will not be forgotten
in *the* end,
the poor will not perish
in *the* end.

9:20 Rise up, Lord!
Let man not be comforted.
Let nations be judged
in your sight.
9:21 Appoint, Lord,
a law-giver over them!
May nations know
that they are *only* men,
9:22 that what You, Lord,
pulled far back from,
You will despise in times
of tribulation.[17]

---

[17] In RSV and KJV, this verse marks the beginning of Psalm 10. Hereafter, Vulgate chapter numbering differs from the

9:23 As long as *the* lawless
are proud,
the poor *one* will be burned.
Yet they will be captured
in *the* counsels
which they follow.
9:24 Because *a* sinner
is praised in his soul's desires,
the treacherous is blessed.
9:25 *A* sinner has exasperated
the Lord, according to
the multitude of his rages.
He does not seek.
9:26 *There* is no God
in his sight.
His ways are stained
at all times.
He takes away
Your judgment from his face.
He will be ruled
by all his enemies.

9:27 For he said in his heart,
"I will not be moved
from generation to generation,
without harm."
9:28 *His* mouth
is full of cursing,
bitterness, and deceit.
Hard work and pain *are*
under his tongue.
9:29 His sits in ambush,
with *the* rich in hiding,

---

standard numbering in English language Bibles.

so he can kill *the* innocent.
9:30 His eyes will watch
the poor *one*.
He waits, hidden.
Like *a* lion in his den,
he lies in wait,
so he can plunder *the* poor,
snatch away *the* poor one
while he tears him *apart*.

9:31 He will be humiliated
in his *own* trap.
He will bend himself over
and fall,
when he has ruled *the* poor.
9:32 For he said in his heart,
"God forgot.
He turned His face away,
so He could not see
in *the* end."

9:33 Rise up, Lord God!
Raise Your hand
and do not forget *the* poor!
9:34 For how *the* lawless
has provoked God!
For he said in his heart,
"He won't require *it*."
9:35 You see, because You
consider hard work and pain,
so You can hand them
over into Your hands.
The poor one
is abandoned to You.
You were *the* orphan's helper.
9:37 Break *the* sinners' arm!

The malignant
will seek his sin,
and will not find it.

9:37 *The* Lord will reign
in eternity,
and in *the* age of ages.
You will destroy
nations from Your land.
9:38 *The* Lord heard
the poor's desire.
His ears heard
their heart's preparation.

9:39 Judge *the* orphan
and *the* humble,
so man can do no more
to magnify himself
over *the* land!

Psalm 10:1 (KJV Ps 11)
To *the* end.
A psalm of David.

10:2 I trust in *the* Lord.
How can you say to my soul,
"Fly away like *a* sparrow
to *the* mountains?
10:3 "For, look!
Sinners stretched out *the* bow.
They readied their arrows
in *the* quiver –
to fire them in darkness
at *the* honest in heart.
10:4 "For what you
completed,
they destroyed.
But what does
the fair *one* have?"

10:5 *The* Lord *is* in
His holy temple.
The Lord is in *the* sky,
His throne.
His eyes consider *the* poor.
His eyelids question
men's children.
10:6 *The* Lord questions
fair and lawless.
He hates *the* soul
who delights in betrayal.
10:7 He will rain on sinners
snares of fire and sulphur.
A stormy wind
will be their cup's portion,
10:8 because *the* Lord is fair,

and delights in fairness.
His appearance looks
on equity.

Psalm 11:1 (KJV Ps 12)
To *the* end, for *the* eighths.
A psalm of David.

11:2 Make me secure, Lord,
because *the* holy has faltered,
because truths are lessened
among men's children!
11:3 They spoke pointlessly –
each one to his neighbor.
Lying lips *are* in *the* heart,
and they spoke from *the* heart.

11:4 May *the* Lord
utterly ruin all lying lips,
every boasting tongue –
11:6 those who said,
"We will glorify our tongue.
Our lips are ours.
Who is our Lord?"

11:7 "Because of
the needy one's misery
and *the* poor one's groan,
now I will rise up,"
says *the* Lord.
"I will place in security.
I will lead faithfully in it."

11:8 *The* Lord's eloquence
is pure silver's eloquence –
examined and proved by fire,
purged seven times of earth.
11:8 You, Lord, will save us
and keep us,
from this generation

and in eternity.
11:9 *The* lawless stalk
back and forth.
According to Your height,
You have multiplied
men's children.[18]

Psalm 12:1 (KJV Ps 13)
To *the* end.
A psalm of David.

How long, Lord?
Will You forget me
to *the* end?
How long are You turning
Your face away from me?
12:2 How long will I
put counsel in my soul,
pain in my heart, every day?
12:3 How long
will my enemy
be lifted up over me?

12:4 Look! Hear me,
Lord my God!
Enlighten my eyes,
lest at any moment
I fall asleep in death –
12:5 so my enemy
may not say,
"I prevailed against him."
Those who trouble me
will be joyful if I am moved.

12:6 But I have hoped
in Your mercy.
My heart will rejoice
in Your security.
I will sing to *the* Lord,
who gives me good.
I will sing psalms
to *the* Lord Most High's
name.

---

[18] Compare to RSV: *On every side the wicked prowl, as vileness is exalted among the sons of men.*

Psalm 13:1 (KJV Ps 14)
To *the* end.
A psalm of David.

The fool says in his heart,
"There is no God."
They are corrupt
and have become disgusting
through their pursuits.
There is no one
who will do good!
There is not even one!

13:2 *The* Lord looked down
from *the* sky
at men's children,
so He could see
if *there* is an intelligent *one*,
or *one* seeking God.

13:3 All alike turned away.
They became useless.
There is not one
who will do good.
There is not even one.
Their throat is *an* open grave.
They carry on deceitfully
with their tongues.
Asp venom *is* beneath
their lips,[19]
whose mouth is full
of cursing and bitterness,
whose feet *are* swift
to spilling blood.
Regret and unhappiness
are in their ways,
and they have not known
peace's way.
God's fear is not
before their eyes.

13:4 Don't they know,
all who work treachery,
who devour my people
like *a* piece of bread?
13:5 They have not
invoked *the* Lord
in that place.
They walked fearfully
where *there* was no fear,
13:6 because God is among
the fair generation.
You confused *the* counsel
of *the* powerless,
yet God is his hope.[20]

13:7 Who will give Israel
security from Sion?
When *the* Lord turns aside
His people's captivity,
Jacob will exult
and Israel will be joyful.

---

[19] Asps are deadly snakes from northern Africa.

[20] Compare to RSV: *You would confound the plans of the poor, but the LORD is his refuge.*

Psalm 14:1 (KJV Ps 15)
A psalm of David.

Lord, who will live
in Your tent,
or who will rest
on Your holy mountain?
14:2 One who goes in
without fault,
and who works fairness –
14:3 who speaks truth
in his heart,
who has not carried on fraud
with his tongue,
or done harm to his neighbor,
and does not accept ill rumors
against his neighbors.

14:4 *The* malignant
is pulled down
to nothing in His sight,
but He glorifies *those*
who fear *the* Lord –
one who swears
to his neighbor
and does not lie –
14:5 who hasn't lent
his money at usury,
and did not accept bribes
against *the* innocent.

One who does these
will not be moved in eternity.

Psalm 15:1 (KJV Ps 16)
A title's inscription
by David himself.

Preserve me, Lord,
because I hoped in You!
15:2 I said to *the* Lord,
"You are my Lord,
because You have no need
of my goods."
15:3 He glorified me
by *the* holy *ones*
who are in His land.
All my desires *are* in them.

15:4 After they hurried,
their infirmities
were increased.
I will not gather
in their bloody assembly,
nor will I remember
their name with my lips.

15:5 *The* Lord *is*
my inheritance's portion,
and my cup.
You are *the* One
who restores my inheritance
to me.
15:6 Lines have fallen
in clarity for me,
for my inheritance
is clear to me.

15:7 I will bless *the* Lord,
who gives me understanding

from above.
Even till night my insides
have rebuked me.[21]

15:8 I always made provision
for the Lord in my sight.
Because He is
at my right *hand*,
I will not be moved.
15:9 Because of this,
my heart is happy.
My tongue has exulted
above measure,
and my flesh will rest in hope.
15:10 For You
will not abandon
my soul to *the* inferno,
nor will You cause
Your holy One
to see corruption.
You notice me.
You made life's ways.
You will fill me with joy
with Your appearance.
Delight *is* in Your right hand,
even to *the* end.

---

[21] Compare to RSV: *I bless the LORD who gives me counsel; in the night also my heart instructs me.* The Latin uses "kidneys" instead of "heart."

Psalm 16:1 (KJV Ps 17)
A prayer of David.

Hear my fairness, Lord!
Listen to my plea!
Perceive my prayer
with Your ears –
not *offered* from deceitful
lips!
16:2 May my judgment
come forth from Your face.
May Your eyes look
on equitable *causes*.

16:3 You proved my heart.
You visited by night.
You examined me by fire,
and treachery is not found
in me.
16:4 So my mouth would not
speak human works,
I have kept difficult ways,
according to Your lips' words.
16:5 Make my walk whole
in Your paths,
so my footsteps won't moved!

16:6 I called because You,
God, heard me.
Incline Your ear to me
and hear my words!
16:7 Make Your mercies
marvelous,
through which You make
those hoping in You secure!

16:8 Guard me
like your eye's pupil,
from those resisting
Your right *hand*!
You will protect me
under Your wing's shadow,
16:9 from *the* face
of *the* lawless
who have afflicted me.
My enemies have surrounded
my soul against me.
16:10 They closed up
their fat.
Their mouth spoke pride.[22]
16:11 Throwing me out,
now they surrounded me.
They set their eyes
to bend *me* down
to *the* ground.
16:12 They have taken me
like *a* lion prepared for prey,
and like *a* young lion
living in secret *places*.

16:13 Rise up, Lord!
Go before him
and overthrow him!
Rescue my soul, Your spear,
from *the* lawless –
16:14 Your hands, Lord,
from enemies!
Keep them away
from *the* land's little ones
during their life!
Their womb is filled
from Your hiding place.
They are satisfied by children,
and leave their possessions
to their little ones.

16:15 But I will appear
in fairness in Your sight.
I will be satisfied
when Your glory appears.

---

[22] Compare to RSV: *They close their hearts to pity; with their mouths they speak arrogantly.*

Psalm 17:1 (KJV Ps 18)
To *the* end,
for *the* Lord's servant, David,
which he spoke to *the* Lord,
the words of this song,
on *the* day when *the* Lord
rescued him from *the* hand
of all his enemies,
and from Saul's hand,
and he said,

17:2 I will delight in you,
Lord my strength.
17:3 *The* Lord
is my foundation,
my refuge, and my liberator,
my God, my helper.
I will hope in Him,
my protector,
my well-being's power
and my sustainer.
17:4 Praising, I will
invoke *the* Lord,
and will be secure
from my enemies.

17:5 Death's pains
surrounded me.
Betrayal's torrents disturbed
me.
17:6 *The* inferno's pains
surrounded me.
Death's snares went
before me.
17:7 When I was
hard pressed,
I invoked *the* Lord.
I cried out to my God.
He has heard my voice
from His holy temple.
My outcry in His sight
will enter into His ears.

17:8 *The* land is moved
and has trembled.
The mountains' foundations
are troubled and disturbed
because He is angry
with them.
17:9 Smoke ascended
in His wrath,
and fire flashed forth
from His face.
Coals blazed forth from Him.
17:10 He bent *the* skies
and came down,
gloom beneath His feet.
17:11 He mounted
the cherubim[23] and flew.
He flew on *the* wind's wings.
17:12 He made shadows
His hiding place around Him,
gloomy waters in *the* air's
clouds His tent.
17:13 Lightning *flashed*

---

[23] The cherubim were angelic beings thought to surround God's throne. See Isaiah 37:16: *O LORD of hosts, God of Israel, who art enthroned above the cherubim, thou art the God, thou alone, of all the kingdoms of the earth; thou hast made heaven and earth.*

before *Him,* in His sight.
His clouds passed over –
hail and burning coals.

17:14 *The* Lord thundered
from *the* sky.
The Most High
gave His voice –
hail and burning coals.
17:15 He sent out arrows
and scattered them.
He multiplied lightning
and troubled them.
17:16 *The* waters'
sources appeared,
and *the* foundations
of *the* land's circle
were laid open,
at Your rebuke, *O* Lord –
by *the* breathing in
of Your anger's breath.

17:17 He sent
from *the* heights
and received me.
He raised me up out
of many waters.
17:18 He will rescue me
from my mightiest enemies,
and from those who hated me,
because they were
strengthened against me.
17:19 They went before me
on my trouble's day,
and *the* Lord became
my protector.

17:20 He led me out
into *a* broad *place.*
He will make me secure
because He wanted me.

17:21 *The* Lord will repay me
according to my fairness.
He will repay me
according to my hands' purity.
17:22 For I kept
the Lord's ways,
nor did I turn away lawless
from my God.
17:23 Because all His
judgments
are in my sight.
I have not pushed
His right *decrees*
away from me.
17:24 I will be
without stain with Him.
and I will watch closely,
far from my treachery.

17:25 *The* Lord will repay me
according to my fairness,
and according to
my hands' purity
in His eyes' sight.

17:26 With *the* holy,
You will be holy.
With *the* innocent,
You will innocent.
17:27 With *the* chosen
You will be chosen.

With *the* perverse
You will pervert –
17:28 because You will make
a humble people secure,
and will humiliate
the proud eye.

17:29 Because You
light my lamp,
Lord my God,
You light up my shadows.
17:30 Because in You
I am rescued from temptation,
in my God I will climb
over *a* wall.

17:31 My God –
His way is unpolluted.
The Lord's word
is proven by fire.
He is *the* protector
of all who hope in Him.
17:32 For who *is* god
besides *the* Lord?
Who *is* god
besides our God –
17:33 God,
who surrounds me
with strength
and made my way spotless –
17:34 who completed
my steps like deer,
and stands me
on *the* heights –
17:35 who teaches my hands
in battle!

You place *a* bronze bow
in my arms.
17:36 You gave me
Your well-being's protection.
Your right arm sustained me.
You discipline corrects me
to *the* end.
Your discipline –
this will teach me.
17:37 You broadened
my steps beneath me,
and my footsteps
have not weakened.

17:38 I will pursue
my enemies and take them.
I will not turn back
until they are destroyed.
17:39 I will smash them,
nor will they be able
to stand.
They will fall
beneath my feet.

17:40 You have braced me
with strength for war.
You have overturned
under me those rising up
against me.
17:41 You gave me
my enemies' backs,
and destroyed those
who hated me.
17:42 They cried out
but no one was *there*
who could make them secure.

They cried out to *the* Lord,
but He did not listen to them.

17:43 I will grind them up
like dust before *the* wind's face.
I will crush them
like *the* streets' gravel.

17:44 Rescue me
from people's contradictions!
You will establish me
at *the* nations' head.
17:45 People whom
I did not know served me.
At *the* ear's hearing
they obeyed me.
17:46 Strangers' children
lied to me.
Strangers' children grew old
and grew lame
because of their paths.

17:47 *The* Lord lives,
and my God *is* blessed.
May my well-being's God
be lifted up!
17:48 God, who
gives me revenge
and subdues peoples
under me,
is my liberator from
the nations' wrath.
17:49 He will lift me up
from those rising up
against me,
and rescue me
from *the* lawless.

17:50 Because of this,
I will confess to You
among nations, Lord.
I will chant *a* psalm
to Your name –
17:51 magnifying
His King's well-being,
and making mercy
to David, His Christ,
and to his seed in *the* age.

Psalm 18:1 (KJV Ps 19)
To *the* end.
A psalm of David.

18:2 *The* skies
tell God's glory.
Its foundation makes known
His hands' works.
18:3 Day brings up word
to day
and night indicates knowledge
to night.
18:4 *There* are no voices
nor conversations,
whose voices are not heard.
18:5 Their sound
has gone out to all *the* land,
and their words
to *the* land's circle's limits.

18:6 He placed His tent
in *the* sun, and he,
like *a* groom
leaving his marriage bed,
will exult like *a* giant
to run his course.
18:7 His leaving *is*
from *the* highest,
and his return *is*
even to *the* highest,
nor is *there* anyone
who hides himself
from his heat.

18:8 *The* Lord's Law
is flawless, converting souls.
The Lord's testimony
is trustworthy,
lending wisdom to little ones.
18:9 *The* Lord's right *decrees*
are correct,
making hearts joyful.
The Lord's precept *is* clear,
enlightening eyes.
18:10 Fear of *the* Lord
is holy, enduring forever.
The Lord's judgments
are true,
proved in themselves –
18:11 more desirable
than gold
and very precious stones,
sweeter than honey
and honeycomb.

18:12 Indeed Your slave
keeps them.
A great reward
is in keeping them.

18:13 Who
understands offenses?
Cleanse me
from my hidden *ones*!
18:14 Spare Your slave
from strangers!
If they do not rule me,
then I will be without stain.
I will be cleansed
from *the* greatest offense.
18:15 And my mouth's words
will be as if acceptable.

My heart's meditation
will be in Your sight always,
O Lord my helper
and my redeemer.

Psalm 19:1 (KJV Ps 20)
To *the* end.
A psalm of David.

19:2 May *the* Lord hear you
in trouble's day.
May *the* name of Jacob's God
protect you.
19:3 May He send you help
from His holy *place*,
and watch over you
from Sion.
19:4 May He remember
all your sacrifices,
and may your burnt offering
be made fat.
19:5 May He give to you
according to your heart,
and strengthen all your
counsel.

19:6 We will be happy
in your security.
We will be made greater
in our God's name.
19:7 May *the* Lord fulfill
all your requests.
Now I have known
that *the* Lord made
His Christ secure.
He will hear him
from His holy sky.
God's right hand's safety
is in might.

19:8 These *trust* in chariots

and these in horses,
but we will invoke
the Lord our God's name.
19:9 They are bound
and have fallen.
We, truly, have risen
and are standing up straight.

19:10 Lord,
make *the* king secure,
and hear us on *the* day
we invoke You!

Psalm 20:1 (KJV Ps 21)
To *the* end.
A psalm of David.

20:2 Lord, *the* king
will be happy
in Your strength,
and will exult fiercely
over Your security.
20:3 You have given him
his soul's desire,
and have not deceived him
though his lips' will.
20:4 Because You went
before him
in sweetness's blessings,
You placed *a* crown
of precious stone on his head.
20:5 He asked life of You,
and You gave him
length of days in *this* age,
and in *the* age of ages.

20:6 His fame *is* great
in Your security.
You will place fame
and great beauty over him,
20:7 because You will give
him blessing in *the* age
of ages.
You will make Him rejoice
in joy with Your appearance,
20:8 because *the* King
hopes in *the* Lord.
In *the* Most High's mercy,
he will not be moved.

20:9 May your hand be found
by all Your enemies!
May Your right hand find
all who hate You!

20:10 You will make them
like *a* glowing oven
in *the* time
of Your appearance.
The Lord will trouble them
in His wrath.
Fire will devour them.
20:11 You will
destroy their fruit
from *the* land,
their seed from among
men's children,
20:12 because they turned
away from You.
They plotted harmful counsel,
which they weren't able
to bring about,
20:13 because You
put them behind.
You will prepare their face
among Your survivors.

20:14 Be exalted, Lord,
in Your strength!
We will sing and praise
Your strengths.

Psalm 21:1 (KJV Ps 22)
To *the* end,
for *the* morning's assumption.
A psalm of David.

21:2 God, my God,
look at me!
Why have You
abandoned me?
My offenses' words
are far away from health.
21:3 My God,
I will call by day,
yet You will not hear,
and by night,
and foolishness *is* not
with me.

21:4 But You live in *the* holy,
O Praise of Israel.
21:5 Our fathers
hoped in You.
They hoped,
and You freed them.
21:6 They called to You
and were made secure.
They hoped in You
and were not confused.

21:7 But I am *a* worm
and not *a* man,
a disgrace among men
and *an* outcast among people.
21:8 All who see me
mock me.
They spoke to me

with their lips.
They shook their head.
21:9 "He hoped in the Lord.
Let *God* rescue him!
Let *God* make him secure,
if He wants him!"

21:10 *Yet* You are *the* One
who took from *the* womb –
my hope from my mother's
breasts.
21:11 I was cast on You
from *the* uterus.
You are my God
from my mother's womb.

21:12 Do not abandon me,
because trouble
is my neighbor,
because *there* is no one
who helps!
21:13 Many young bulls
surrounded me.
Many fat bulls besieged me.
21:14 Their mouth
opened over me,
like *a* tearing and roaring lion!
21:15 I am poured out
like water.
All my bones are scattered.
My heart became
like melted wax
in *the* middle of *my* chest.
21:16 My strength dried up
like *a* pot's lid.
My tongue stuck to my jaws.

You led me into death's filth.

21:17 For many dogs
surrounded me.
A malignant council
seized me.
They stabbed my hands
and my feet.
21:18 They numbered
all my bones.
Truly, they stared at
and inspected me.
21:19 They divided
my clothing among
themselves,
and cast lots over my robe.

21:20 But You, Lord, do not
take away my help!
Look to my defense!
21:21 Rescue my soul
from *the* spear,
and my only *life*
from dogs' hands!
21:22 Save me from
the lions' mouth,
and my humility
from *the* unicorns' horns.

21:23 I will tell my brothers
Your name.
I will praise You
in *the* assembly's midst.
21:24 *You*
who fear *the* Lord,
praise Him!

Magnify Him,
all Jacob's seed!
21:25 Let all Israel's seed
fear Him,
because He has not
scorned or despised
the poor *one's* plea,
nor has He turned His face
away from me.
When I called Him,
He heard me.
21:26 My praise *is* with You
in *the* great assembly.
I will pay my promises
in *the* sight of all
who fear You.

21:27 *The* poor will eat
and be filled,
and will praise *the* Lord.
Those who seek Him --
their hearts will live
in *the* age of ages.
21:28 All *the* land's ends
will remember,
and will turn to *the* Lord.
All nations' families
will worship in His sight.
21:29 Because power
is God's,
He will rule nations.

21:30 All *the* land's fat *ones*[24]
have eaten and bowed down
in His sight.
All who go down
to *the* land will fall.
21:31 Yet my soul –
it will live.
My seed will serve Him.

21:32 *The* coming generation
will be told about *the* Lord,
and will announce
His fairness to *a* people
yet to be born,
whom *the* Lord has made.

---

[24] The "fat of the earth" are the rich.

Psalm 22:1 (KJV Ps 23)
A psalm of David.

The Lord will guide me.
Nothing will be lacking to me.
22:2 In *a* place of pasture –
there He established me.
He taught me
over refreshing waters.
22:3 He converted my soul.
He led me over fair paths,
for His name's sake.

22:4 Even if I walk
in *the* midst
of death's shadow,
I will not fear harm
because You are with me.
Your rod and Your staff –
these consoled me.
22:5 You prepared *a* table
in my sight,
against those who afflict me.
You anointed my head
with oil.
My cup, inebriating,
how clear it is!

22:6 Your mercy
will follow me
all my life's days,
so that I will live
in *the* Lord's house
through length of days.

Psalm 23:1 (KJV Ps 24)
A psalm of David,
first of *the* Sabbath.

The land is *the* Lord's
and its abundance,
the land's circle
and all who live in it,
23:2 because He
established it over *the* sea,
and prepared it over rivers.

23:3 Who climbs up
to *the* Lord's mountain,
or who will stand
in His holy place?
23:4 *The* innocent in hand
and clean of heart,
who has not grasped
his soul vainly,
or sworn deceitfully
to his neighbor!
23:5 He will receive
blessing from *the* Lord,
and mercy from God,
His savior.
23:6 This is *the* generation
of those who seek Him –
who seek Jacob's God's face.

23:7 Lift up your gates,
Princes!
Be lifted up, eternal gates!
And glory's King will enter!
23:8 Who is glory's King?
The Lord, strong and mighty!

The Lord, mighty in battle!

23:9 Lift up your gates,
Princes!
Be lifted up, eternal gates!
And glory's King will enter!
23:10 Who is glory's King?
Strength's Lord –
He is glory's King!

Psalm 24:1 (KJV Ps 25)
A psalm of David.

I lifted up my soul
to You, Lord.
24:2 My God, I trust You.
May I not be ashamed,
24:3 nor may my enemies
mock me –
for all who sustain You
will not be dismayed.

24:4 May all *those*
practicing treachery
without cause be dismayed.
Show me Your ways, Lord,
and teach me Your paths!
24:5 Guide me in Your truth
and teach me,
because You are God,
my savior,
and I have sustained You
all day!

24:6 Remember
Your compassion, Lord,
and Your mercy,
because they are from *the* age!
24:7 Do not remember
my youth's offenses,
or my ignorance!
Be mindful of me, Lord,
according to Your mercy,
according to Your goodness!

24:8 *The* Lord

is pleasing and honest.
Because of this,
He will give *the* Law
to those failing in *the* way.
24:9 He will guide
the gentle in judgment.
He will teach
the peaceful His ways.
24:10 All *the* Lord's ways
are mercy and truth
to those seeking His covenant
and His testimony.

24:11 According to
Your name, Lord,
atone even for my sin,
for *it* is great.[25]

24:12 Who is *the* man
who fears *the* Lord?
God will set
His law before him,
in *the* way which He chooses.
24:13 His soul
will live in good.
His seed will inherit
the land.
24:14 *The* Lord
is *the* foundation
of those who fear Him.
His testament will be
made clear to them.

24:15 My eyes are always
to *the* Lord,
because He will pull
my feet out of traps.
24:16 Watch over me,
and have mercy on me,
because I am alone and poor!
24:17 My heart's troubles
are multiplied.
Rescue me from necessities![26]
24:18 See my humiliation
and my hard work,
and let go of all my offenses!
24:19 Look on my enemies
because they are multiplied!
They hated me
with *a* betraying hatred.
24:20 Guard my soul
and rescue me!
May I not be ashamed
that I trusted in You.

24:21 *The* innocent
and honest stayed beside me,
because I sustained You.
24:22 God, free Israel
from all his tribulations!

---

[25] The Psalmist asks God to propitiate, to make ritual atonement, forgive his sins. Apparently, nothing less that formal atonement can appease a justifiable divine vengeance.

[26] To rescue "from necessities" is to deliver someone from the tyranny of having to worry about the daily essentials of life: food, clothing, shelter, and such.

Psalm 25:1 (KJV Ps 26)
A psalm of David.

Judge me, Lord,
because I have walked
in my innocence!
I will not be weakened,
hoping in *the* Lord.
25:2 Prove me, Lord,
and test me!
Try my insides
and my heart.[27]

25:3 Because Your mercy
is before my eyes!
I have pleased in Your truth.
25:4 I did not sit
with *the* useless council.
I will not enter in
with betrayal's workers.
25:5 I hated
the malignant gathering,
and will not sit
with *the* lawless.
25:6 I will wash my hands
among *the* innocent,
and walk around Your altar,
Lord,
25:7 so I
can hear praise's voice,
and tell all Your wonders.

25:8 Lord, I delighted
in Your house's beauty,
and Your glory's
dwelling place.
25:9 Do not destroy
my soul with *the* lawless,
or my life with bloody men,
25:10 in whose hands
are betrayals!
Their right hand
is full of bribes,
25:11 but I have walked
in my innocence.
Buy me back
and have mercy on me!
25:12 My foot stood straight
in *the* gatherings.

I will bless You, Lord.

---

[27] Compare to RSV: *Prove me, O LORD, and try me; test my heart and my mind.*

Psalm 26:1 (KJV Ps 27)
Of David, before he was
sealed.

The Lord *is* my light
and my security.
Whom will I fear?
The Lord *is*
my life's protector.
Of whom will I be afraid?

26:2 When *those* hating me
come close to me
so they can eat up my flesh –
who trouble me
and *are* my enemies –
they weakened
and have fallen.
26:3 If armies
form against me,
my heart will not fear.
If battle rises against me,
I will hope in this.

26:4 I have asked one *thing*
of *the* Lord.
This I will seek –
that I may live
in *the* Lord's house
all my life's days –
that I may see *the* Lord's will
and visit His temple.
26:5 For He
hid me in His tent
on *a* harmful day.
He protected me
in His dwelling's
hidden *place*.
26:6 He lifted
me up on *a* rock,
and now, He has lifted up
my head over my enemies.
I walked around and burned
the protesting victim
in *God's* tent.[28]
I will sing and chant *a* psalm
to *the* Lord.

26:7 Hear my voice, Lord,
by which I cried out!
Have mercy on me
and hear me!
26:8 My heart said to You,
"My face has sought *You*."
I will seek Your face, Lord.

26:9 Don't turn Your face
away from me,
or turn back from Your slave
in Your anger!
Be my helper!

Do not abandon me
or despise me,
God my savior!
26:10 For my father
and my mother
abandoned me,

---

[28] The psalmist describes the process of offering an animal in sacrifice to the Lord.

but *the* Lord took me up.

26:11 Place *the* law
in me, Lord, in Your way,
and guide me in right paths,
because of my enemies!
26:12 Do not hand me over
to souls afflicting me,
because treacherous witnesses
have risen up against me!
Yet iniquity is *a* lie to itself.

26:13 I am confident
of seeing *the* Lord's good
in *the* living's land.
26:14 Wait for *the* Lord!
Live manfully!
Let your heart be comforted,
and sustain *the* Lord!

Psalm 27:1 (KJV Ps 28)
To David.

I will cry out to You, Lord,
My God, do not be silent,
unless You be silent to me
and I be like those
who go down into *the* pit!
27:2 Hear my petitions' voice
while I pray to You –
while I raise my hands
toward Your holy temple!

27:3 Do not hand me over
together with sinners,
with those who work betrayal!
Do not let me be destroyed
with those who speak peace
with their neighbor,
but harms are in their hearts!

27:4 Give to them
according to their actions,
according to *the* worthlessness
of their inventions!
Grant to them according to
their hands' works!
Repay their vengeance
to them,
27:5 because they have not
understood *the* Lord's works!
You will destroy them
in his hands' works,
and not build them up.

27:6 *The* Lord *is* blessed,

because He has heard
my petitions' voice.
27:7 *The* Lord *is* my helper
and my protector.
My heart hoped in Him,
and I am helped.
My flesh will prosper again
and I will confess Him
from my will.
27:8 *The* Lord *is*
His people's strength.
He is *the* protector
of His Christ's well-being.

27:9 Make
your people secure,
and bless Your inheritance!
Rule them and lift them up,
even in eternity!

Psalm 28:1 (KJV Ps 29)
A psalm of David,
in *the* Tabernacle's
completion.

Bring to *the* Lord,
God's children,
bring to *the* Lord young rams!
28:2 Bring to *the* Lord
glory and honor!
Bring to *the* Lord
His name's glory!
Adore *the* Lord
in His holy *place's* courtyard!

28:3 *The* Lord's voice
is over *the* waters.
The God of majesty thunders,
Lord over many waters.
28:4 *The* Lord's voice
thunders in strength.
The Lord's voice
thunders in magnificence.
28:5 *The* Lord's voice
is shattering cedars.
The Lord smashes
Lebanon's cedars.
28:6 *The* Lord
will smash them
like Lebanon's calf,
and like *the* delight
of *the* unicorn's child.

28:7 *The* Lord's voice *is*
cutting through flames of fire.

28:8 *The* Lord's voice *thunders,*
striking *the* desert.
The Lord will move
the desert of Kadesh.[29]
28:9 *The* Lord's voice
is preparing *the* deer.
He will open *the* thick woods,
and in His temple all say,
"Glory!"

28:10 *The* Lord makes
the flood to inhabit.
The Lord will be enthroned,
King in eternity.
28:11 *The* Lord will give
His people strength.
The Lord will bless
His people in peace.

Psalm 29:1 (KJV Ps 30)
A psalm of song,
at *the* dedication
of David's house.

29:2 I will lift You up, Lord,
because You received me,
and did not delight
in my enemies over me.
29:3 Lord my God,
I cried out to You
and You healed me.
29:4 Lord, You led my soul
out of *the* inferno.
You saved me from those
going down into *the* pit.

29:5 Sing psalms to *the* Lord,
His holy ones!
Confess His holiness's
memory,
29:6 because wrath
is in His indignation,
and life *is* in His will!
Weeping will linger
at evening,
yet joy *breaks through*
toward morning.

29:7 But I said
in my abundance,
"I will not be moved
in eternity."
29:8 Lord, in Your will
You supplied
my beauty's strength.

---

[29] The "desert of Kadesh" is in the northeast portion of the Sinai peninsula, through which God led the Israelites during the Exodus.

You turned Your face away
and I became troubled.
29:9 I will
call out to You, Lord,
and make my plea to my God.
29:10 What use *is there*
in my blood,
while I go down
to corruption?
Will dust confess You
or announce Your truth?

29:11 *The* Lord heard
and had mercy on me.
The Lord became my helper.
29:12 You converted
my lament into joy for me.
You tore my sackcloth
to pieces,[30]
and surrounded me
with happiness,
29:13 so my glory
can sing to You,
and I will not be ashamed.
O Lord my God,
I will confess You in eternity.

---

[30] Sackcloth was worn as a sign of mourning.

Psalm 30:1 (KJV Ps 31)
To *the* end.
A psalm of David.

30:2 I hoped in You, Lord.
May I not be dismayed
in eternity.
In Your fairness, set me free!
30:3 Incline Your ear to me!
Hurry and rescue me!
Be to me God *the* protector,
refuge's house,
that You may make me
secure!
30:4 For You are my strength
and my refuge.
For Your name's sake,
You will lead me
and nourish me.

30:5 You lead me
out of this trap
which they hid against me,
because You are my protector.
30:6 I will trust my spirit
into Your hands.
You bought me back,
Lord, God of truth.

30:7 You hated
those watching
unnecessary vanities,
but I hoped in *the* Lord.
30:8 I will exult
and be happy
in Your mercy,

because You saw
my humility.
You saved my soul
from necessities,
30:9 nor did You close me up
in enemies' hands.
You made my feet stand
in *a* spacious place.

30:10 Have mercy
on me, Lord,
because I am troubled!
My eye is disturbed
by anger –
my soul and my belly,
30:11 because my life
grew faint in pain,
and my years in groaning.
My strength is weakened
in poverty,
and my bones are troubled.
30:12 I became *a* reproach
to all my enemies –
greatly to my neighbors –
fear to those who know me.
Those who saw me outside
ran away from me.
30:13 I was
given over to oblivion,
like *the* dead.
I became like
a smashed vessel
from *the* heart.
30:14 For I have heard
many vicious attacks
from those living nearby,
while they gathered
against me.
They were consoled
to take away my soul.

30:15 But I hoped
in you, Lord.
I said, "You are my God.
30:16 "My lots
are in Your hands.
Rescue me from
my enemies' hand,
from those who persecute me!
30:17 "Light up Your face
over Your slave!
Make me secure
in Your mercy!"
30:18 Lord,
may I not be dismayed,
because I called on You.
May *the* lawless be ashamed
and led to *the* inferno.
30:19 May deceitful lips
be made mute,
who speak iniquity
against *the* fair,
in pride and in abuse.

30:20 How great *is* Your
sweetness's multitude, Lord,
which You have hidden
for those fearing You –
which You have perfected
for those who hope in You
in men's children's sight!
30:21 You hide them

in Your face's secret *place*
from men's disturbance.
Your protect them
in *Your* tent
from tongues' contradiction.
30:22 *The* Lord *is* blessed.
He has magnified
His mercy to me
in *the* fortified city.

30:23 But I said
in my mind's excess,
"I am thrown away
from Your eyes' face."
Therefore, You heard
my prayers' voice
while I cried out to You.
30:24 Delight in *the* Lord,
all His holy ones,
because *the* Lord
requires truth,
and will repay abundantly
those who act proudly!
30:25 Live manfully,
and let your heart
be comforted,
all who hoped in *the* Lord!

Psalm 31:1 (KJV Ps 32)
By David's understanding.

Blessed *are those*
whose betrayals are forgiven,
whose sins are covered.
31:2 *A* man *is* blessed
to whom *the* Lord
will not charge sin,
nor is deceit in his spirit.
31:3 Because I kept silent,
my bones grew old
while I cried out all day.
31:4 For day and night
Your hand was heavy on me.
I was turned back
in my distress
while *a* thorn pierced me.
31:5 I made my offense
known to You.
I did not hide my unfairness.
I said, "I will confess
my *own* unfairness
to *the* Lord, against myself ."
You forgave my sin's
lawlessness.

31:6 Because of this,
every holy *one* will pray
to You at *a* favorable time.
Even so, in *a* flood
of many waters,
they will not come close
to him.
31:7 You are my refuge
from *the* tribulation

which surrounded me.
My Exultation, rescue me
from those who surround me!
31:8 "I will give you
understanding,
and instruct you in *the* way
by which you may walk.
I will fix My eyes on you.
31:9 "Don't be like
a horse or mule,
which is not intelligent!
Restrain their jaws
with muzzle and bit,
who do not come close
to you!"

31:10 Many beatings
fall on sinners,
but mercy will surround one
who hopes in *the* Lord.
31:11 Be happy in *the* Lord,
and exult, *you* fair!
Boast *in Him*,
all *you* upright in heart!

Psalm 32:1 (KJV Ps 33)
A psalm of David.

Exult, *you* fair, in *the* Lord!
Praise befits *the* honest.
32:2 Confess to *the* Lord
on guitar!
Sing psalms to Him
on *the* ten-stringed harp!
32:3 Sing Him *a* new song!
Sing psalms well,
with passion,
32:4 because
the Lord's Word is right,
and all His works
are done in faithfulness!
32:5 He delights in
mercy and judgment.
The land is full
of *the* Lord's mercy.

32:6 By *the* Lord's Word,
skies were founded,
and all their strength
by His mouth's Spirit,
32:7 gathering
the sea's waters
as if in *a* wine skin,
and putting *them*
in *the* abysses' treasuries .
32:8 Fear *the* Lord,
all *the* land!
May all *the* world's
inhabitants
be moved by Him,
32:9 because He spoke

and they were made.
He commanded
and they were created.

32:10 *The* Lord scatters
the nations' counsel.
He rebukes
the peoples' thoughts,
and rebukes *the* princes'
counsel.
32:11 But *the* Lord's counsel
endures in eternity,
His heart's thoughts *remain*
in generation after generation.
32:12 *The* nation whose God
is *the* Lord *is* blessed –
His people, whom He chose
as *an* inheritance for Himself.

32:13 *The* Lord
has looked down
from *the* sky.
He has seen all
men's children.
32:14 From His
prepared dwelling,
He looked down over all
who live in *the* land –
32:15 *He*, who made
their hearts individually,
who understands
all their works.

32:16 *A* king is not saved
by much power,
and *a* giant will not be saved
by his strengths' multitude.
32:17 *A* horse is
deceitful for safety,
for he will not be saved
by its strength's abundance.

32:18 Look, *the* Lord's eyes
are on those who fear Him,
who hope in His mercy,
32:19 that He may rescue
their souls from death,
and feed them in famine.
32:20 Our soul
sustains *the* Lord,
because He is our helper
and protector.[31]
32:21 For our heart
will be happy in Him.
We have hoped
in His holy name.
32:22 Let Your mercy
be over us, Lord,
to *the* extent that we
have hoped in You.

---

[31] Note the use of "Our soul" here. It is a collective soul. "Our heart" is used similarly in the following verse.

Psalm 33:1 (KJV Ps 34)
By David, when he changed
his face before Abimelech,
and he sent him away
and he left.[32]

33:2 I will bless *the* Lord
at all times.
His praise *remains*
always in my mouth.
33:3 My soul
will be praised in *the* Lord.
Let *the* gentle hear
and be happy!
33:4 Magnify *the* Lord
with me!
Let us lift up His name
in itself!

33:5 I sought *the* Lord
and He heard me.
He rescued me
from all my troubles.
33:6 Come near to Him
and be enlightened.
Your faces will not be
dismayed.
33:7 This poor *one* cried out
and *the* Lord heard him,
and saved him
from all his troubles.

33:8 *The* Lord's angel
will be *a* fortified wall
around those who fear Him,
and will rescue them.
33:9 Taste and see
that *the* Lord is pleasing.
A man who hopes in Him
is blessed.
33:10 Fear *the* Lord,
all His holy ones,
because *there* is no lack
to those who fear Him.
33:11 *The* rich were
in need and hungry,
but those seeking *the* Lord
will not be lacking
in any good.

33:12 Come, children!
Hear me!
I will teach you
the Lord's fear.
33:13 Who is *the* man
who wants life,
who wants to see good days?
33:14 Keep your tongue
away from harm,
and do not let your lips
speak deceit.
33:15 Turn away from harm
and do good.
Seek peace and pursue it!

33:16 *The* Lord's eyes
are on *the* fair,
and His ears *listen*
to their prayer.

---

[32] Abimelech may have been King of the Philistine city of Gath in David's time.

33:17 *The* Lord's face *is*
against those working harm,
so He can destroy
their memory from *the* land.
33:18 *The* fair cried out
and *the* Lord heard them.
He freed them
from all their troubles.
33:19 *The* Lord is
beside those who
are troubled in heart.
He will save
the spiritually humble.
33:20 Fair *people's*
troubles *are* many,
yet He freed them
from all of them.
33:21 *The* Lord guards
all their bones.
Not one of these
will be shattered.
33:22 *A* sinner's death
is dismal,
and those who hate *the* fair
will fall short.
33:23 *The* Lord buys back
His slaves' souls.
All who hope in Him
will not fall short.

Psalm 34:1 (KJV Ps 35)
By David himself.

Judge those
who hate me, Lord!
Attack those attacking me!
34:2 Take up
armor and shield
and rise up to help me!
34:3 Throw *Your* spear
and shut up those
who are persecuting me!
Say to my soul,
"I am your security!"

34:4 Let those
seeking my soul
be dismayed and awestruck.
Let those contemplating
my harm be turned back
and dismayed.
34:5 Let them
be made like dust
before *the* wind's face,
and *the* Lord's angel
closing them in.
34:6 Let their way be made
shadowy and slippery,
and *the* Lord's angel
pursuing them,
34:7 because they hid
their traps' destruction
against me without cause!
They accused my life
for no reason.
34:8 Let *the* trap they ignored

come to them,
and *the* deception
which he hid trap him.
May he fall in *the* same trap.

34:9 But my soul
will exult in *the* Lord.
It will delight
over His security.
34:10 All my bones say,
"Lord, who is like You –
rescuing *the* poor from *a* hand
stronger than him –
the needy and destitute
from those tearing him
apart?"
34:11 Treacherous witnesses
are standing up.
They questioned me
about what I did not know.
34:12 They paid me back
harm for good,
my soul's barrenness.

34:13 But when
they were troubled at my side,
I clothed myself in mourning.
I humbled my soul in fasting.
My prayer in my heart
will be changed.
34:14 Like *a* neighbor,
like our brother,
so I made myself acceptable.[33]
Like one weeping
and grieved,
thus I humbled myself.
34:15 Yet they were
happy against me
and gathered together.
Wounds were gathered
against me,
and I did not know.
34:16 They were scattered.
Not repentant, they tested me.
They mocked me
with derision.
They ground their teeth
over me.

34:17 Lord, when
will You see?
Restore my soul
from their malice,
my only *life* from lions!
34:18 I will confess to You
in *the* great assembly.
I will praise You
amidst *the* mass of people.
34:19 May those
who oppose me
not be too happy over me –
liars who hate me
without cause,
who wink *their* eyes,

---

[33] "I made myself acceptable" implies performing the rituals of repentance before God, both in outward observance and in the heart.

34:20 for they certainly spoke
peacefully to me,
yet, speaking
in *the* land's wrath,
they plotted lies.
34:21 They opened
their mouths wide against me
and said, "Good! Good!
Our eyes have seen!"

34:22 You saw, Lord.
Don't be silent, Lord,
or pull back from me!
34:23 Rise up
and understand my judgment,
my God and my Lord,
in my cause!
34:24 Judge me
according to Your fairness,
Lord my God!
Let them not be
too happy over me.
34:25 Let them not say
in their hearts,
"Good! Good to our souls."
May they not say,
"We have eaten him up."

34:26 May they be ashamed
and embarrassed together,
who congratulated themselves
at my misfortunes.
May they be dressed
in confusion and awe
who speak great against me.
34:27 May those who
desire my fairness
exult and be happy.
May those who want
His servants' peace
always say,
"Magnify the Lord!"

34:28 My tongue
will consider Your fairness,
Your praise, all day.

Psalm 35:1 (KJV Ps 36)
To *the* end,
by David, *the* Lord's slave.

35:2 *The* unfair spoke,
that he might fall short
in himself.
God's fear is not
before his eyes,
35:3 because he acted
deceitfully in His sight,
si his betrayals
could be found *and* hated.
35:4 His mouth's words
are betrayals and lies.
He did not want
to understand,
so that he might live well.
35:5 He brooded
over betrayal in his bed.
He stood up in every way
that isn't good,
yet he has not hated malice.

35:6 Lord, Your mercy
is in *the* sky
and Your truth
even to *the* clouds,
35:7 Your fairness *is*
like God's mountains.
Your judgment *is*
like *the* abyss.
You will save
many men and cattle,
35:8 just as You multiplied
Your mercy, *O* God.
But men's children will hope
in Your wings' shelter.
35:9 They will be drunk
from Your house's fertility.
You will give them water
from Your will's torrent.[34]
35:10 For life's fountain
is with You.
In Your light we see light.

35:11 Stretch out Your mercy
to those who know You,
and Your fairness
to those whose hearts
are upright!
35:12 May *the* foot
of *the* proud not come to me,
and sinners' hands not
move me.
35:13 They fell there,
who worked treachery.
They were pushed back
and could not stand.

---

[34] Ensuring agricultural fertility played a huge role in the religious practices of both the Israelites and their neighbors. The root of the words for "fertility" and "breasts" is the same. The word "torrent" indicates the value of a reliable water source in a semi-arid land.

Psalm 36:1 (KJV Ps 37)
Of David himself.

Do not long to imitate
the malignant,
or let yourself be jealous
of those working treachery,
36:2 for like hay,
they quickly dry up,
and just like leaves of grass,
they quickly wither!

36:3 Hope in *the* Lord,
and do good,
and live in *the* land,
and you will be fed
in its riches!
36:4 Delight in *the* Lord
and He will give you
your heart's petitions!
36:5 Open your way
to *the* Lord and hope in Him,
and He will make *it*!

36:6 He will lead out
your fairness like light,
and your judgment
like midday.
36:7 Submit yourself
to *the* Lord and pray to Him!
Do not desire to imitate one
who prospers in his way,
a man doing injustices!

36:8 Cease from wrath
and leave behind fury!
Don't imitate just to do harm,
36:9 because those
who do harm will be
wiped out!
But those sustaining
the Lord –
they will inherit *the* land.

36:10 In just *a* little while,
a sinner will not exist.
You will seek his place
and will not find *him.*
36:11 But *the* gentle
will inherit *the* land,
and will delight
in peace's multitude.

36:12 *The* sinner will
watch *the* fair
and grind his teeth
against him.
36:13 But *the* Lord
will laugh at him,
because He sees that
his day will come.

36:14 Sinners
unsheathed *the* sword
and aimed their arrow,
so they could destroy
the poor and weak,
so they could slaughter
the upright in heart.
36:15 May their sword
enter their own heart,
and their bow be shattered!

36:16 *A* small *amount*
to *the* fair
is better than sinners'
many riches,
36:17 because sinners' arms
will be broken,
but *the* Lord strengthens
the fair.
36:18 *The* Lord has known
the days of *the* sinless.
Their inheritance
will be in eternity.
36:19 They
will not be dismayed
in *a* harmful time.
In days of famine
they will be filled.

36:20 For sinners will perish.
The Lord's enemies,
soon after they were
honored and exalted,
were scattered,
blowing away like smoke.
36:21 *A* sinner will borrow
and not pay back,
but *a* fair *one* has mercy
and will give.
36:22 For those blessing him
will inherit *the* land,
but those cursing him
will be ruined.

36:23 With *the* Lord,
men's way are guided,
and he will desire *God's* way.

36:24 When he falls
he will not be crushed,
because *the* Lord
puts His hand *under him*.

36:25 I was young
and grew old,
and I have not seen
the fair *one* abandoned,
or his seed begging bread.
36:26 All day long
he has mercy and provides.
His seed will be in blessing.

36:27 Turn back from harm
and do good,
and live in *the* age of ages,
36:28 for *the* Lord
loves judgment
and will not abandon
His holy *ones!*
They will be preserved
in eternity.
The unfair will be punished
and *the* lawless seed
will perish.
36:29 But *the* fair
will inherit *the* land,
and will live on it
in *the* age of ages.

36:30 *The* fair *one's* mouth
will meditate wisdom,
and his tongue
will speak judgment.
36:31 His God's law

is in his heart.
His steps will not be
undermined.

36:32 *A* sinner
looks at *a* fair *one,*
and seeks to destroy him.
36:33 But *the* Lord
will not abandon him
into his hands,
or condemn him
when He judges him.

36:34 Wait for *the* Lord
and keep His way,
and He will lift you up,
so that you take *the* land
by inheritance!
When sinners perish,
you will see.
36:35 I saw *the* lawless,
lifted up and tall
like Lebanon's cedars.
36:36 And I passed by
and, look, he was not *there*!
I sought him
and his place was not found.
36:37 Guard *the* innocent
and see to equity,
for these are *a* peaceful man's
legacies!

36:38 But *the* lawless
will be destroyed together.
The legacies of *the* lawless
will perish!

36:39 But *the* security
of *the* fair *is* from *the* Lord.
He is their protector
in times of trouble.

36:40 *The* Lord
will help them and free them,
and rescue them from sinners.
He will make those
who have hoped in Him
secure.

Psalm 37:1 (KJV Ps 38)
A psalm of David,
in *the* Sabbath's
remembrance.

37:2 Lord,
do not argue with me
in Your fury,
or correct me in Your anger,
37:3 for Your arrows
are fixed in me!
You strengthened
Your hand over me.
37:4 *There* is
no health in my flesh
from Your anger's face.
There is no peace in my bones
from my sins' face,
37:5 for my treacheries
have mounted up
over my head.
Like *an* oppressive weight
they are loaded down
over me.
37:6 My scars have rotted
and are corrupted
from *the* face
of my stupidities.
37:7 I have become wretched
and bent down to *the* end.
I have walked all day,
discouraged.
37:8 For my privates
are filled with mocking.
There is no health in my flesh.
37:9 I am afflicted
and I am humiliated.
I have bellowed too much
from my heart's moans.

37:10 Lord,
all my desire is before You.
My groaning is not hidden
from You.
37:11 My heart is troubled.
My strength has left me.
My eyes' light itself
is not with me.
37:12 My friends
and my neighbors
have come near
and stood against me.
Those who were beside me
have stood far away.
37:13 Those
who were seeking
my life caused violence.
Those who sought harm
spoke vanities against me.
All day long they meditated
on lies.
37:14 But I, like *the* deaf,
did not hear.
I was like *the* mute,
not opening his mouth.
37:15 I became like
a man not hearing,
and not having answers
in his mouth.

37:16 For I
hoped in You, Lord.

You will hear me,
Lord my God,
37:17 because I said,
"May my enemies
never be too happy over me
when my feet are moved."

They have spoken
great *harms* against me.
37:18 For I
am prepared for wounds,
and my pain is always
in my sight.
37:19 For I
will tell my treachery,
and I will consider my sin.
37:20 But my enemies
will live and are strengthened
against me.
Those who hate me
treacherously are multiplied.
37:21 Those who pay back
harm for good tore me down,
because I sought *the* good.

37:22 Do not abandon me,
O Lord my God!
Do not pull back from me!
37:23 Aim toward my help,
O my health's Lord!

Psalm 38:1 (KJV Ps 39)
To *the* end, to Idithun.
A song of David.

38:2 I said,
"I will guard my ways,
that I not fall short
through my tongue."

I placed my mouth
under guard
when *a* sinner stood up
against me.
38:3 I became silent
and was humbled.
I grew quiet, apart from good,
and my pain was renewed.
38:4 My heart
grew hot inside me,
and fire will blaze forth
in my meditation.

38:5 I said in my tongue,
"Make my end
known to me, O Lord,
and what *the* number
of my days is –
so I may know
what is lacking to me!"
38:6 Look, You established
my days' measures.
My substance
is like nothing before You.
All *the* same,
every living man is vanity.
38:7 Even so, man passes

through in appearance,
yet is troubled
even for no reason.
He gathers treasures,
yet does not know
for whom he will gather them.

38:8 And now,
what is my expectation?
Isn't it *the* Lord?
My substance is with You.
38:9 Rescue me
from all my betrayals!
You have given me
a fool's shame.
38:10 I kept silent
and didn't open my mouth
because You did *it*.
38:11 Take Your beatings
away from me!
38:12 I
have been destroyed
in rebukes
from Your hand's strength.
Because of betrayal,
You have corrected man,
and made his soul dry up
like *a* spider's web.
Nevertheless, each man
is troubled vainly.
38:13 Hear my prayer, Lord!
Understand my petition
with *Your* ears!
Do not silence my tears,
because I am *an* stranger
with You,
a pilgrim, like all my fathers!
38:14 Send me back,
that I may be refreshed,
before I go away
and will be no more!

Psalm 39:1 (KJV Ps 40)
To *the* end,
a psalm of David.

39:2 I waited
eagerly for *the* Lord,
and He reached out to me.
39:3 He heard my prayers
and led me out of misery's pit
and grief's dregs.
He stood my feet on *a* rock
and guided my steps.
39:4 He put
a new song in my mouth,
a song to our God.
Many will see and fear
and hope in *the* Lord.
39:5 *A* man *is* blessed,
whose hope is
the Lord's name.
He did not look
on foolishness
and false insanities.

39:6 You, Lord my God,
made Your wonders many.
No one is like You
in Your thoughts.
I spoke and said,
"They are multiplied
beyond number."
39:7 You did not want
sacrifice and offering,
but You perfected hearing
in me.
Not even for sin
have You demanded
a burnt offering.

39:8 Then I said,
"Look, I come.
In *the* beginning of *a* book
it is written of me,
39:9 "that I might
do Your will, my God."

I desired even Your law
in *the* middle of my heart.
39:10 I told Your fairness
in *a* great gathering.
Look, I will not
restrain my lips.
Lord, You knew.
39:11 I did not hide
Your fairness in my heart.
I spoke of Your truth
and Your security.
I did not hide
Your mercy and Your truth
from *a* great council.

39:12 But you, Lord,
do not make Your compassion
far from me!
Your mercy and Your truth
have always sustained me.
39:13 For harmful *people*
who can't be numbered
have surrounded me.
My treacheries
have seized me,
and I couldn't even see.

They are multiplied more
than *the* hairs of my head.
My heart has abandoned me.
39:14 May *it*
please You, Lord
that You rescue me!
Look down, Lord, to help me!
39:15 Let them be dismayed
and awestruck at once
who seek my soul
that they may carry it away.
Let them be turned back
and awestruck
who want harm for me.
39:16 Let them receive
their confusion suddenly
who say over me,
"Good! Good!"
39:17 Let them exult
and be joyful over You –
all who seek You.
Let them always say,
"The Lord be magnified,"
who delight in Your security.

39:18 But I
am *a* beggar and poor.
The Lord is concerned for me.
You are my helper
and my protector.
My God, do not delay!

Psalm 40:1 (KJV Ps 41)
To *the* end.
A psalm of David.

40:2 One who understands
about *the* needy and poor
is blessed.
The Lord will free him
in harm's day.
40:3 May *the* Lord
conserve him
and give him life,
make him blessed in *the* land,
and not hand him over
into his enemies' soul.
40:4 May *the* Lord
bring him help
on his pains' bed.
You have turned over
all his cover in his illness.

40:5 I said, "Lord,
have mercy on me!
Heal my soul,
because I have sinned
against you!"

40:6 My enemies have
spoken harms against me.
"When will he die
and his name perish?"
40:7 And if one came in
so he could visit *me,*
he spoke vainly.
His heart gathered
treachery to itself.

He went outside
and spoke *harshly*.
40:8 They
murmured against me
in *the* thing itself.
All my enemies
plotted harm against me.
40:9 They set up
lying words against me.
"One who sleeps
won't be strengthened,
will he, so he can get up
again?"

40:10 For even
a man of my peace,
in whom I hoped,
who ate my bread,
has increased *his* plotting
against me.

40:11 But You, Lord,
have mercy on me!
Raise me up,
and I will repay them!
40:12 In this I knew
that You wanted me,
because my enemies
will not rejoice over me.
40:13 You received me
according to my innocence,
and strengthened me
in Your sight in eternity.
40:14 *The* Lord,
God of Israel, is blessed
from *the* age
and to *the* age!

Let it be, let it be!

End of Book One

Book Two

Psalm 41:1 (KJV Ps 42)
To *the* end, in understanding.
Of Korah's sons.[35]

41:2 Just as *a* deer longs
for springs of water,
so my soul longs
for You, God.
41:3 My soul thirsted
for *the* mighty *and* living God.
When will I come
and appear before God's face?
41:4 My tears
were bread for me,
day and night,
while *it* is said to me daily,
"Where is your God?"

41:5 I have remembered this,
and poured out my soul in me.
For I will cross over
to Your wondrous
dwelling place,
even to God's *own* house,
in exulting
and confessing's voice –
feasting's sound!

41:6 Why
are you sad, my soul,
and why do you trouble me?
Hope in God,
for I will confess to Him,
my face's security!

41:7 My God,
my soul is troubled
to me myself.
Because of this,
I will remember You
from Jordan's land
and Hermon,
from *the* small mountain.[36]
41:8 Abyss invokes to abyss
in Your waterfalls' voice.
All Your heights
and Your floods
have passed over me.
41:9 *The* Lord
has commanded
His mercy by day
and His song by night.
Prayer to my life's God
is with me.

41:10 I will say to God,
"You are my sustainer.
Why have You forgotten me?

---

[35] Korah was a descendant of Levi, Israel's priestly tribe. The Levites were responsible for the operation first of the Lord's Tent of Meeting, then later of the Temple. Korah himself has a distinctive role in the Exodus story, beginning at Exodus 16.

[36] The Jordan River forms the border between present-day Israel and Jordan. Mount Hermon dominates the border region between Israel, Syria, and Lebanon. The "land of Jordan and Hermon," then, is in what is now northeastern Israel.

Why do I advance in sadness
while my enemy afflicts me,
41:11 "while
my bones are broken?
Those who trouble me
have reproached me,
while they say to me each day,
'Where is Your God?'"

41:12 Why
are you sad, my soul,
and why do you trouble me?
Hope in God,
for I will confess Him,
my face's security
and my God!

Psalm 42:1 (KJV Ps 43)
A psalm of David.

Judge me, God,
and discern my cause
against *an* unholy nation!
Rescue me from treacherous
and deceitful man!
42:2 For You, God,
are my strength.
Why have You
pushed me away?
Why do I walk in sadness
while *the* enemy afflicts me?
42:3 Send out Your light
and Your truth!
These have led me out
and brought me
into Your holy sanctuary,
and into Your tents.

42:4 I will enter
toward God's altar,
to God who makes
my youthfulness glad.
I will confess to You
on guitar, God, my God.

42:5 Why
are you sad, my soul,
and why do you trouble me?
Hope in God,
for I will confess Him still,
my face's security
and my God.

Psalm 43:1 (KJV Ps 44)
To *the* end,
of Korah's sons,
to understanding.

43:2 God,
we have heard with our ears.
Our fathers have told us
the work which You did
in their days, in ancient days.
43:3 Your hand
destroyed nations
and planted them.
You afflicted peoples
and expelled them.
43:4 For they did not possess
the land by their sword,
and were not saved
by their arm –
but by Your right hand
and Your arm,
and Your face's light,
for You were pleased
with them.

43:5 You Yourself
are my King and my God,
who commands security
for Jacob.
43:6 In You, we will expose
our enemies to *the* spear.
In Your name,
we will look down on those
rising up against us.
43:7 For I
will not hope in my bow.
My sword will not save me.
43:8 For You have saved us
from those afflicting us.
You dismayed those
who hate us.
43:9 We will
rejoice in God all day.
We will confess Your name
in *the* age.

43:10 But now You have
pushed us back
and dismayed us.
You have not gone out
with our armies.
43:11 You turned us back
after our enemies.
Those who hated us
tore us apart for themselves.
43:12 You gave us over
like sheep *sold* for meat.
You have scattered us
among nations.
43:13 You sold
Your people without price.
There was no great *cost*
in our exchange.
43:14 You made us
our neighbors' scorn,
mockery and derision
to those who live around us.
43:15 You
made us like *the* nations,
a wagging of heads
among peoples.
43:16 All day my shame

is against me.
My face's confusion
overwhelms me,
43:17 from *the* voice of those
rebuking and interrupting –
from *the* enemy's face
and those persecuting us.

43:18 All this came over us,
though we have not
forgotten You,
or carried on treacherously
in Your covenant.
43:19 Our heart
did not pull back from You,
yet You turned our paths
away from Your way.
43:20 For You humiliated us
in affliction's place.
Death's shadow covered us.

43:21 If we have forgotten
our God's name,
or if we stretched out
our hands to *a* strange god,
43:22 won't God
require this?
For He knows
the heart's hidden *depths*.
For on Your account
we are killed all day.
We are considered
like sheep for slaughter.

43:23 Rise up!
Why are You sleeping, Lord?
Rise up!
Do not push *us* back
to *the* end!
43:24 Why have You turned
Your face away?
Why have You forgotten
our poverty and our troubles?
43:25 For our soul
is humiliated in dust!
Our gut is stuck to *the* ground!

43:26 Rise up!
Help us and redeem us,
for Your name's sake!

Psalm 44:1 (KJV Ps 45)
To *the* end,
for those who will be
changed.
Of Korah's sons,
toward understanding.

A song for *the* beloved.

44:2 My heart
has brought up *a* good word.
I speak my works to *the* King.
My tongue is
a scribe's reed pen,
rapidly writing.
44:3 *Your* form *is* beautiful
before men's children.
Grace is spread out
in Your lips,
because God has blessed you
in eternity.
44:4 Strap Your sword
on Your thigh,
O Most Powerful!
44:5 By Your appearance
and Your beauty, also work!
Go forth successfully
and reign for truth's sake –
gentleness and fairness!
Your right hand
will lead You out
marvelously.

44:6 Your arrows *are* sharp
in *the* King's enemies' hearts.
Peoples fall beneath You.

44:7 Your throne, *O* God,
exists in *the* age of ages.
Guidance's rod
is *the* rod of Your rule.
44:8 You
delighted in fairness
and hated treachery.
Because of this, God,
Your God, anointed You
with gladness's oil,
before Your consorts.

44:9 Myrrh, drops, and cassia
fall from Your clothes,
from Your ivory houses,
from which they delighted
You.
44:10 King's daughters
stand in Your honor.
The queen stood
at Your right *hand*,
in *a* gilded gown,
wrapped in embroideries.

44:11 Listen,
daughter, and see!
Incline your ear!
Forget your people
and your father's house!
44:12 *The* King
will desire your beauty,
for He is your Lord,
and they will adore Him.
44:13 Tyre's daughters
will petition before your face
with gifts,

the rich among peoples.
44:14 All his glory,
of *the* king's daughter,
is within, in golden borders.
44:15 Clothed
in embroideries,
virgins will be led
to *the* King after her.
Her neighbors will be brought
to you.
44:16 They will be brought
in joy and exultation.
They will be brought
into *the* King's temple.
44:17 Sons
are born to you
for your fathers.
You will constitute them
princes over *the* land.
44:18 I
will remember your name
in each generation
and generation.
Because of this,
peoples will confess to You
in eternity and in *the* age
of ages.

Psalm 45:1 (KJV Ps 46)
To *the* end,
for Korah's sons,
for *the* hidden ones.

A psalm.

45:2 God
is our refuge and strength,
helper in troubles
which came upon us
overwhelmingly.
45:3 Therefore,
we will not be afraid
while *the* land is troubled
and mountains are moved
in *the* sea's heart.
45:4 *These* have sounded.
Their waters are in turmoil.
Mountains are shaken
in their strength.

45:5 Flowing rivers
make glad God's city.
The Most High
made His dwelling holy.
45:6 God lives in its midst.
It will not be moved.
God will help it early,
at daybreak.
45:7 Nations are disturbed.
Kingdoms *are* bent down.
He gave His voice.
The land moved.
45:8 *The* Lord
of armies *is* with us,

our sustainer, Jacob's God.

45:9 Come and see
the Lord's works,
which He placed *as* wonders
over *the* land,
45:10 taking away wars
to *the* land's end!
He will break *the* bow,
shatter armor,
and burn shields in fire.

45:11 Empty yourselves
and see that I am God!
I will be praised
among nations.
I will be exalted in *the* land.
45:12 *The* Lord with us
is our strength, our sustainer,
Jacob's God.

Psalm 46:1 (KJV Ps 47)
To *the* end,
for Korah's sons.

A psalm.

46:2 Clap
your hands, all nations!
Sing joyfully to God
in exultation's voice!
46:3 For *the* Lord Most High
is terrible, *a* great King
over all *the* land!
46:4 He made peoples
subject to us,
nations beneath our feet.
46:5 He has chosen us
as His inheritance,
Jacob's beauty,
whom He loved.
46:6 God
rose up in jubilation,
the Lord, in *the* trumpet's
voice.

46:7 Sings
psalms to our God!
Sing!
Sing psalms to our King!
Sing psalms!

46:8 God is King
over all *the* land.
Sing psalms wisely!
46:9 God ruled over nations.
God sat on His holy throne.

46:10 *The* nations' princes gathered together with Abraham's God.
The mighty of God's land were lifted up forcefully.

Psalm 47:1 (KJV Ps 48)
A psalm song of Korah's sons, second Sabbath.

47:2 *The* Lord *is* great,
exceedingly worthy of praise,
in God's city –
in His holy mountain.
47:3 *It* is established
by all *the* land's praise,
Sion's mountains,
by *the* northern side,
the great King's city.
47:4 God will be known
in its houses,
when He will sustain her.
47:5 For, look,
kings came together.
They gathered as one.
47:6 Seeing *for* themselves,
they admired *it*.
They were troubled.
They were moved.
47:7 Trembling overtook
them there, pains like
childbirth.

47:8 With fierce wind,
You will shatter
Tharsis's ships.
47:9 As we have heard,
so we have seen
in *the* city
of *the* Lord of armies –
in our God's city.
God founded it in eternity.

47:10 We
received Your mercy,
God, in *the* middle
of Your temple.
47:11 Accord
to Your name, God,
so also *is* Your praise
to *the* land's ends.
Your right hand
is full of fairness.

47:12 Let
Mount Sion be joyful!
Let Judah's daughters exult,
because of Your judgment,
Lord!
47:13 Walk
around Sion and take it in!
Tell of its towers!
47:14 Set
your hearts in its strength
and distribute its houses,
that you may tell it
in another generation!
47:15 For God is here –
our God in eternity
and in *the* age of ages!
He will rule us in *the* age.

Psalm 48:1 (KJV Ps 49)
To *the* end,
of Korah's sons.

48:2 Hear this, all nations!
Perceive with *your* ears,
all who live in *the* world,
48:3 whoever
is born of earth,
men's children as one,
rich and poor!
48:4 My mouth
will speak wisdom,
My heart's meditation
is prudence.
48:5 I will
incline my ear to *a* parable.
I will open my proposition
in psalm.

48:6 Why
will I fear in harm's day?
My heel's treachery
will surround me.
48:7 Those who trust
in their strength's bounty
glory in their riches.
48:8 *A* brother
does not redeem.
A man does *not* redeem.
He will not give God
His appeasement,
48:9 *the* price
of his soul's redemption.
He has worked hard
in eternity,

48:10 and still
he will live to *the* end.
48:11 He will
not see destruction
when he sees *the* wise dying.

The stupid and *the* fool
will perish together,
and leave their riches
to strangers.
48:12 Their tombs will be
their homes in eternity –
their dwellings in generations
and generations.
They have called their names
in their lands.
48:13 Man,
when he was in honor,
did not understand.
He is like dull-minded cattle,
and became like them.

48:14 This way of theirs
is *a* scandal to them.
Afterwards they will be
satisfied by their own mouth.
48:15 Like sheep
they are placed in *the* inferno.
Death will feed on them.
The fair will dominate them
in *the* morning.
Their help will grow old
in *the* inferno,
far from their glory.

48:16 Nevertheless,
God will redeem my soul
from *the* dead's hand,
when He receives me.
48:17 You don't have to fear
when man is made rich,
and when his house's glory
is multiplied.
48:18 For when
he is destroyed,
he will not take
everything away,
nor will his glory
go down after him.

48:19 For his soul
will be blessed in his life.
He will confess to You
when You are kind to him.
48:20 He will enter
to his fathers' generations
in eternity.
He will not see light.

48:21 Man,
when he was in honor,
did not understand.
He is like dull-minded cattle,
He became like them.

Psalm 49:1 (KJV Ps 50)
A psalm of Asaph.[37]

The gods' God,
the Lord has spoken
and called *the* land,
from *the* sun's rising
even to its setting,
49:2 from Sion,
the embodiment
of His beauties
49:3 God
will come openly –
our God –
and will not be silent.
Fire will burn in His sight,
mighty storms around Him.
49:4 He
has called to sky above
and to *the* land,
to discern His people.

49:5 Gather to Him,
His holy ones,
who order His covenant
as more than sacrifices!
49:6 *The* skies
will announce His fairness,
for God is judge.

49:7 "Listen, My people!
I will speak to You, Israel.
I, God, will testify to you.
I am your God.
49:8 "I will not dispute you
over your sacrifices,
for your burnt offerings
are always in My sight.
49:9 "I will not accept
calves from your house,
or male goats
from your flocks,
49:10 "for all *the* forest's
animals are mine –
cattle on *the* mountains,
and oxen.
49:11 "I have known
all *the* sky's birds,
and *the* field's beauty
is mine.
49:12 "If I were hungry,
I would not tell you,
for *the* land's circle
and all its plenty is mine.
49:13 "Will I eat bulls' flesh
or drink goats' blood?

49:14 "Burn to God
the sacrifice of praises
and pay your promises
to *the* Most High!
49:15 "Invoke Me
in trouble's day!
I will rescue you

---

[37] Asaph writes after the destruction of Jerusalem and its temple in 587 B.C.E. His themes involve reminding Israel of God's past acts, invoking again God's supernatural care, and calling God's people to renewed faithfulness and trust under the Covenant. He gives voice to the impulse that gathered Israel's scattered written traditions into one holy book in the dark years of exile.

and you will honor Me.

49:16 But to sinners
God has said,
"Why do you recount
My just works
and take up My covenant
with your mouth?
49:17 "You, truly,
have hated discipline,
and thrown My words behind.
49:18 "If you saw *a* thief,
you ran with him.
You set your portion
with adulterers.
49:19 "Your mouth
overflowed with harm.
Your tongue put together lies.
49:20 "Sitting down,
you spoke against
your brother,
You placed *a* stumbling-block
in front of your mother's
children.
49:21 You
have done these *things,*
and I was silent.
You supposed, wrongly,
that I will be like you.
I will dispute you,
and set My face against you.

49:22 "Understand this now,
you who have forgotten God,
lest He seize *you*
and there be no one
who rescues!
49:23 "You will honor me
with *the* sacrifice of praises.
There is *the* road
by which I will show you
God's security."

Psalm 50:1 (KJV Ps 51)
To *the* end.
A psalm of David,
50:2 when
Nathan *the* prophet
came to him,
when he had gone in
to Bathsheba.[38]

50:3 Have mercy
on me, God,
according to Your
great mercy!
According to Your
compassions' multitude,
erase my betrayal!
50:4 Wash me further
from my treachery!
Make me clean me
from my sin!

50:5 I know my treachery.
My sin is right in front of me.
50:6 To You only
have I sinned,
and done harm before You –
that You may be justified
in your words,
and You may conquer
when You are judged.

50:7 Look, I
was conceived in iniquity.
My mother conceived me
in sins.
50:8 Look, You
have loved truth.
You made known to me
uncertain and hidden *insights*
of Your wisdom.
50:9 You will
sprinkle me with hyssop
and I will be clean.
You will wash me,
and I will be whitened,
whiter than snow.
50:10 You will give joy
to what I hear.
My humiliated bones
will exult with joy.
50:11 Turn
Your face away from my sins!
Erase all my betrayals!
50:12 Create
a clean heart in me, God!
Return *a* right spirit
to my insides!

50:13 Don't throw me out
from Your face!
Don't take Your Holy Spirit
away from me!
50:14 Give me back
Your security's joy!
By *the* principal Spirit
encourage me!

50:15 I will teach
the treacherous Your ways.

---

[38] For the story of David and Bathsheba, see 2 Samuel 11 and 12.

The lawless will be converted
to You.
50:16 Free me
from blood, *O* God,
God of my security!
My tongue will exult
in Your fairness.

50:17 Lord, You
will open my lips.
My mouth will announce
Your praise.
50:18 If You
wanted sacrifice,
certainly I would have
given it.
You will not be pleased
by burnt offerings.
50:19 God's sacrifice
is a troubled spirit.
God will not scorn
a contrite, humbled heart.

50:20 Work favorably
for Sion, Lord,
in Your good will!
May Jerusalem's walls
be built.
50:21 Then You will accept
the fair-minded's offering,
oblations and burnt offerings.
Then they will place
calves on Your altar.

Psalm 51:1 (KJV Ps 52)
To *the* end,
David's understanding,
51:2 when
Doeg *the* Edomite came
and reported to Saul and said,
"David came into
Ahimelech's house."[39]

51:3 Why does he
pride himself in malice,
who is strong in betrayal?
51:4 All day his tongue
plotted unfairness.

You made deceit
like *a* sharp razor.
51:5 You delighted in malice
more than friendliness –
to speak betrayal
more than equity.
51:6 You loved
all rash words, *a* lying tongue.
51:7 Because of this,
God will destroy you
in *the* end.
He will pull you up
and move you out
of *His* tent,
your root from
the living's land.

51:8 *The* fair

---

[39] See 1 Samuel 21:7-22:23.

will see and fear.
They will laugh at him
and say,
51:9 "Look *at the* man
who did not make
God his helper,
but hoped in *the* quantity
of his riches,
and prevailed in his vanity!"

51:10 But I,
like *a* fruitful olive *tree*
in God's house,
hoped in God's mercy
in eternity and in *the* age
of ages.
51:11 I will
confess You in *the* age
for You have made *it*.
I will hope in Your name,
for *it is* good
in Your holy ones' sight.

Psalm 52:1 (KJV Ps 53)
To *the* end,
for intelligence's King,
David.

The empty-headed said
in his heart,
"*There* is no God."
52:2 They are corrupted,
and have become detestable
in treacheries.
There is no one
who does good.
52:3 God looked down
from *the* sky
at men's children,
so He could see
if *an* understanding *one* exists,
or one *who is* seeking God.
52:4 All
turned away together.
They became worthless.
There isn't one
who does good.
There isn't even one!

52:5 Don't they know,
all who work betrayal –
who devour My people
like *a* piece of bread?
52:6 They have not
invoked God there.
They shook fearfully
where *there* was no fear,
for God scattered their bones
who pleased *only* men.

They were mixed together
because God despised them.

52:7 Who will give Israel
security from Sion?
When God turns back
His people's captivity,
Jacob will exult
and Israel will be happy.

Psalm 53:1 (KJV Ps 54)
To *the* end, in songs,
David's understanding,
53:2 when
Ziph's men had come
and said to Saul, "Isn't David
hiding among us?"[40]

53:3 God, in Your name
make me secure!
Judge me in Your strength!
53:4 God, hear my prayer!
With *Your* ears,
perceive my mouth's words!
53:5 For strangers
have risen up against me.
The mighty have sought
my soul.
53:6 Yet look,
the Lord helps me!
The Lord *is* my soul's
sustainer.
53:7 He will turn away *the*
harm my enemies *intended*.
In Your truth, destroy them!

53:8 I will sacrifice
to You willingly.
I will confess to Your name,
O Lord, for *it* is good.
53:9 For You
have rescued me
from all my trouble.

---

[40] See 1 Samuel 23:14ff.

My eye has looked down
on all my enemies.

Psalm 54:1 (KJV Ps 55)
To *the* end, in songs,
David's understanding.

54:2 *O* God,
hear my prayer
and do not despise
my petition!
54:3 Understand me
and hear me!
I am saddened
in my discipline.
I am troubled
54:4 by *an* enemy's voice,
a sinner's trouble.
They have turned
to betrayals against me.
They are disturbed
in anger against me.
54:5 My heart
is troubled inside me.
Death's dread
has fallen on me.
54:6 Fear and trembling
came over me
Darkness touched me.
54:7 I said,
"Who will give me
wings like *a* dove,
so I can fly away
and find peace?"

54:8 Look,
I withdrew running!
I waited in solitude.
54:9 I waited for Him

who made me secure –
from *a* cowardly spirit,
and from *the* storm.

54:10 Throw
them down, *O* Lord!
Divide their tongues,
for I have seen
betrayal and contradiction
in *the* city!
54:11 Day and night,
He will surround it –
against its walls.
Betrayal and hard work
are in its midst,
54:12 and unfairness.
Usury has not passed away
from its streets, or deceit.
54:13 For if *the* enemy
had cursed me,
I would have endured anyway.
If one who hated me
had spoken great *threats*
against me,
perhaps I would have
hidden myself from him.

54:14 Yet you
are a man of one mind,
my commander
and my familiar *friend*.
54:15 who, together with me,
captured sweet food
in God's house.
We have walked together
in one accord.

54:16 May death
come over them!
May they go down alive
into *the* inferno,
for worthlessness
is in their dwellings
among them!

54:17 But I
called out to God
The Lord will save me.
54:18 Evening,
morning, and midday,
I will tell and announce.
He will hear my voice.
54:19 He will buy back
my soul in peace
from those who
come close to me –
for they were with me
among many.

54:20 God,
who is before *the* ages,
will hear and humble them.
For repentance is not
with them.
They have not feared God.
54:21 He
stretches out His hand
in retribution.
They contaminated
His covenant.
54:22 They are divided
by His face's anger.
His heart has come close.

His words are softer than oil,
yet they are spears.

54:23 Throw
your care on *the* Lord
and He will nourish you.
He will not give uncertainty
to *the* fair forever.
54:24 Truly, God,
You lead them
into *a* well of ruin.
Bloody and deceitful men
will not live out
half their days.
But I will hope in You,
O Lord.

Psalm 55:1 (KJV Ps 56)
To *the* end,
for *a* people who have drifted
far from holiness.

Of David,
in *an* inscription's title,
when Strangers' Friends
had him in Gath.[41]

55:2 Have
mercy on me, God,
for man has
trampled me all day!
Attacking, he
has troubled me.
55:3 My enemies
have trampled me all day.
Many are making war
against me.
55:4 From
day's height, I will fear.
Truly, I will hope in You.
55:5 I will
praise my words in God.
I hoped in God.
I will not fear.
What can flesh do to me?

55:6 All day they will curse
my words against me.
All their counsel *is* in harm.
55:7 They will settle down.
They will hide themselves.

---

[41] See 1 Samuel 21:10-15.

They will watch my heel,
the same way they sustained
my soul.

55:8 You will
make them secure for nothing.
Shatter peoples, *O* God,
in wrath!
55:9 I told You my life.
You placed my tears
in Your sight,
as well as in Your promise.
55:10 Then my enemies
will be turned back,
in whatever day I invoke You.
Look, I have known
that You are my God.

55:11 I will
praise *the* word in God.
In *the* Lord I will
praise *a* speech.
I have hoped in God.
What can man do to me?
55:12 Your promises
are in me, *O* God,
which I will repay.
Praises *are* to You.
55:13 For You rescued
my soul from death,
my feet from slipping,
so I can delight before God
in *the* living's light.

Psalm 56:1 (KJV Ps 57)
To *the* end,
that You not destroy David,
in *a* title's inscription,
when he fled from
Saul's face into *a* cave.[42]

56:2 Have
mercy on me, *O* God!
Have mercy on me,
for my soul trusts in You!
I will hope
in Your wings' shadow.
until betrayal passes over.
56:3 I will cry out
to God Most High –
God who worked
good for me.

56:4 He sent
from *the* sky and freed me.
He gave those trampling me
over to shame.
God sent His mercy
and His truth,
56:5 and rescued my soul
from *the* young lions' midst.
I slept, troubled
for men's children.
Their teeth?
Armor and arrows!
Their tongue *is a* sharp sword.

---

[42] This story begins at 1 Samuel

56:6 May God be lifted up
above *the* skies,
His glory in all *the* land!

56:7 They
prepared *a* trap for my feet.
They bent my soul down.
They dug *a* pit
in front of my face.
Yet they fell in it.

56:8 My heart
is prepared, *O* God.
My heart *is* prepared.
I will sing and chant psalms.

56:9 Rise up, my Glory!
Rise up, psalter and guitar!
I rise up early.
56:10 I will confess to You
among peoples, *O* Lord.
I will chant psalms to You
among nations.
56:11 For Your mercy
is made larger,
even to *the* skies,
and Your truth *lifted up*
to *the* clouds.

56:12 May God
be lifted up above *the* skies,
and His glory over
all *the* land!

Psalm 57:1 (KJV Ps 58)
To *the* end,
that David may not
be destroyed,
in *a* title's inscription.

57:2 If, truly,
you by all means
speak fairness,
judge men's children!
57:3 For in *the* heart
you work betrayals.
Your hands put together
unfairness in *the* land.

57:4 Sinners are alienated
from *the* vulva.
They wander away
from *the* womb.
They have spoken
false *judgments*.
57:5 Their fury *is*
in *the* likeness of snakes.
Like *a* deaf asp,
their ears *are* stopped up.
57:6 *They* will not hear
the snake charmer's voice,
or *the* spells of one
chanting wisely.

57:7 God
will break their teeth
in their mouth.
The Lord will shatter
the lions' molars.
57:8 They

will come to nothing,
like rushing water.
He stretches out His bow
until they are weakened.
57:9 Like wax that melts,
they will be taken away.
Fire has fallen.
They have not seen *the* sun.
57:10 Before your thorns
understood *the* bramble –
as if living, as if in anger –
He overwhelms you.

57:11 *The* fair will be happy
when he sees vindication.
He will wash his hands
in *the* sinner's blood.
57:12 Man will say,
"By all means,
if *there* is fruit to *the* fair,
there is equally *a* God
judging them in *the* land."

Psalm 58:1 (KJV Ps 59)
To *the* end,
that you may not
destroy David,
in *a* title's inscription,
when Saul sent and guarded
his house, that he might
kill him.[43]

58:2 Rescue me
from my enemies, *O* God!
Free me from those
rising up against me!
58:3 Rescue me from those
working betrayal!
Save me from bloody men!
58:4 For, look,
they captured my soul!
The mighty rushed in at me.
58:5 I hurried away –
not because of my treachery
or my sin, *O* Lord –
but because of *their* iniquity.
I arranged *my escape*.

58:6 Get up
to meet me and see!
You, Lord God,
God of Israel's strength,
stretch out and visit
all nations!
Do not have mercy on all
who work betrayal!
58:7 They will turn back

---

[43] See 1 Samuel 19:11-18

at evening.
They will suffer
hunger like dogs.
They will walk around
the city.
58:8 Look! They will speak with their mouth,
yet *a* sword *is* in their lips.
For who has heard?

58:9 You, Lord,
will mock them.
You will reduce all nations
to nothing.
58:10 I will
keep my strength toward You,
for God *is* my sustainer.
58:11 My God –
His purpose will go
before me.
58:12 God
will make me known,
above my enemies.
Do not kill them,
lest my people forget!
Scatter them in Your strength
and lay them aside,
O Lord, my protector!

58:13 Their mouth's offense
is their lips' words.
May they be captured
in their pride!
They will be denounced
for their cursing and lies.
58:14 At *the* end,
in anger at *the* end,
they will cease to exist.
They will know
that God rules Jacob
to *the* land's ends.
58:15 They
will turn back at evening.
They will suffer
hunger like dogs.
They will walk around
the city.
58:16 They
will be scattered,
finding food.
Then, if they aren't satisfied,
they will complain.

58:17 But I
will sing Your strength,
and will exult early
in Your mercy.
You have become
my sustainer and my refuge
in trouble's day.
58:18 My helper –
I will sing psalms to You,
for God, You are
my sustainer, my mercy.

Psalm 59:1 (KJV Ps 60)
To *the* end,
for those who will be
changed,
in *a* title's inscription,
David, in teaching,
59:2 when
Syrian Mesopotamia
and Syria of Soba
were set on fire,
and Joab turned back
and struck twelve thousand
in *the* Valley of Salt.[44]

59:3 O God,
You turned us back
and destroyed us.
You were angry,
yet You were merciful to us.
59:4 You moved *the* land
and troubled it.
Heal its grief,
because it was moved!
59:5 You have shown
Your people hardship.
You watered us
with remorse's wine.
59:6 You have given
those fearing You *a* sign,
so they can flee
from *the* bow's face,
so Your beloved
can be freed.
59:7 Make secure

by Your right *hand*,
and hear me!

59:8 God has spoken
in His holy *place*.
"I will be happy,
and I will divide Shechem,
and measure out
the Valley of Tents.
59:9 "Gilead is mine.
Manasses is mine.
Ephraim *is* my head's
strength.
Judah *is* my King.
59:10 "Moab is my hope's jar.
I will stretch my shoe
in Edom.
Foreigners are subject to me."

59:11 Who will lead me
into *the* fortified city?
Who will lead me
even into Edom?
59:12 *Will it* not
be You, O God,
who turned us back,
and has not gone out, God,
among our armies?

59:13 Give us
help against trouble!
Help from man is vain.
59:14 In God
we will build *an* army.
He will lead
those troubling us to nothing.

---

[44] See 2 Samuel 8:3.

Psalm 60:1 (KJV Ps 61)
To *the* end, in hymns,
of David.

60:2 Hear,
O God, my petition!
Listen to my prayer!
60:3 From *the* land's ends
I cried out to You,
while my heart was anxious.
You lifted me up to *a* rock.
You led me out.
60:4 You
have become my help,
my strong tower against
the enemy's face.

60:5 I will live
in Your tent in *the* age.
I will be protected
in Your *tent* flaps' cover.
60:6 For You, God,
heard my prayer.
You have given *an* inheritance
to those who fear Your name.
60:7 You will add days
upon days to *the* King.
His years *will last*
even in days of generation
after generation.
60:8 He
will remain in eternity
in God's sight.
Who will seek His mercy
and truth?

60:9 I will
chant psalms like this
in Your name
in *the* age of ages,
that I may pay my promises
from day to day.

Psalm 61:1 (KJV Ps 62)
To *the* end, for Jeduthun,
a psalm of David.

61:2 Won't my soul
be subject to God,
for my security *comes*
from Him?
61:3 He *is* my God
and my security, my sustainer.
I will not be moved further.

61:4 How long
do you rush in at *a* man?
All of you are destroying him,
as if *fighting* against
a leaning house
or *a* crumbling wall.
61:5 Nevertheless,
they considered refusing
my price.
I have run in thirst.
They blessed
with their mouth,
yet cursed with their heart.

61:6 Even so, may my soul
be subject to God,
for my patience is from Him.
61:7 For He is my God
and my savior, my helper.
I will not move away.
61:8 My safety
and my fame *are* in God –
my help's God.
My hope is in God.

61:9 Hope in Him,
all *the* people's gathering!
Pour out all your hearts
before Him!
God *is* our helper in eternity.

61:10 Even so,
men's children are worthless.
Men's children *are* liars
in *the* balances,
so they can deceive
to no purpose
in *the* thing itself.
61:11 Do not
hope in treachery!
Do not desire plunder!
If riches abound,
do not put your heart in them!

61:12 God has spoken once.
I have heard these two *times*:
that power *is* God's,
61:13 and to You,
O Lord, is mercy.
You will repay each one
according to his works.

Psalm 62:1 (KJV Ps 63)
A psalm of David, when he
was in *the* Judean desert.

62:2 O God, my God,
I watch for You at daybreak.
My soul thirsted for You.
My flesh *longed* for You
in so many ways.
62:3 In *a* desert land,
impassible and waterless,
thus I have appeared
in *the* holy place before You,
that I might see Your strength
and Your glory.
62:4 Because Your mercy
is better than lives,
my lips will praise You.

62:5 I blessed
you so in my life.
In Your name,
I will lift up my hands.
62:6 As my soul is filled
with fat and abundance,
my mouth will praise
with rejoicing lips.
62:7 If I was mindful of You
on my bed in *the* morning,
I meditated in You,
62:8 because
You were my helper.
In Your wings' shelter
I will rejoice.
62:9 My soul
clung closely to You.
You sustained me by
Your right arm.

62:10 Truly,
they sought my soul vainly.
They will enter into
the land's depths.
62:11 They
will be handed over
to *the* sword's hand.
They will be jackals' portions.

62:12 *The* king, though,
will be happy in God.
All who swear by *God*
will be praised,
because *the* mouth
speaking betrayal is stopped.

Psalm 63:1 (KJV Ps 64)
To *the* end,
a psalm of David.

63:2 Hear my prayer, God,
when I plead!
Rescue my soul
from fear of *the* enemy!

63:3 You protected me
from *a* malignant gathering,
from *a* multitude
of those working betrayal,
63:4 who sharpened
their tongues like swords.
They stretched *the* bow,
a bitter thing,
63:5 so they could shoot
at the faultless in darkness.
63:6 They will
shoot him suddenly
and will not be afraid.
They affirmed *an* opinion
in themselves,
which they haven't told,
so they could hide traps.
They said, "Who will see us?"
63:7 Betrayals are
investigated,
yet the ones inquiring
have faltered under scrutiny.
Man will come near,
a proud heart,
63:8 and God will be exalted.
The little ones' arrows
have become their
misfortunes.
63:9 Their tongues
are weakened against them.
All who saw them
are troubled.
63:10 Every man feared.
They told God's works
and understood His deeds.

63:11 *The* fair
will be happy in *the* Lord,
and will hope in Him.
All those of *an* honest heart
will be praised.

Psalm 64:1 (KJV Ps 65)
To *the* end, *a* psalm of David,
Jeremiah and Haggai's song,
from *the* exiles' word,
when they began to set out.

64:2 *A* hymn
is fitting for You,
O God, in Sion.
A promise will be paid
to You in Jerusalem.
64:3 Hear prayer to You!
All flesh will come.
64:4 Liars' words
prevailed against us,
yet You will atone
for our lawlessness.

64:5 *The* one
You have chosen
and taken up is blessed.
He will live in Your courts.
We will be filled
with Your house's good.
Your temple is holy.
64:6 Wondrous in equity,
hear us – our security's God,
hope of all *the* land's ends,
and of *the* sea far away!
64:7 Preparing mountains
in Your strength,
girded with power,
64:8 *You* are the One
who troubles *the* sea's depths.
Its waves sound.
Nations will be disturbed.

64:9 Those who live
at *the* edges will fear
at Your signs.
You will delight *the* departure
of morning and evening.

64:10 You visited *the* land
and made it drunk.
You multiplied *it*
to enrich her.
God's river is full of water.
You prepared their food,
for such is its preparation.
64:11 Make
its streams drunk!
Multiply its fruit!
By its *water* drops,
the seedling will be happy.
64:12 You will bless
the year's crowns
by Your goodness.
Your fields will be filled
with abundance.
64:13 *The* desert's
spectacular *places*
will flourish.
The hills will be girded
by exultation.
64:14 *The* flock's
rams are dressed.
The valleys will abound
with grain.
They will cry out,
and indeed will chant
a hymn.

Psalm 65:1 (KJV Ps 66)
To *the* end,
a song of psalms,
of rising up.

Shout joyfully to God,
all *the* land!
65:2 Chant
a psalm to His name!
Give glory to His praise!
65:3 Say to God,
"How terrible
are Your works, *O* Lord!
In Your armies' multitude,
Your enemies will lie to You.

65:4 May
all *the* land adore You
and sing psalms to You!
May they chant Your name!
65:5 Come
and see God's works –
terrible in counsels
above men's children,
65:6 *God,* who
changes sea into dry *land*!
They will cross
the river on foot.
There we will be happy
in Him;
65:7 who will rule
in His strength in eternity.
His eyes watch
over *the* nations,
who are frustrated.
Let them not be lifted up
in themselves!

65:8 Bless
our God, *O* nations,
and, hearing, give voice
to His praise –
65:9 *to* Him who placed
my soul in life,
and did not give my feet
into agitation!
65:10 For God proved us.
He examined us by fire,
like silver is examined.
65:11 He led us into *a* trap.
He laid tribulations
on our back.
65:12 He
set men over our heads.
We passed through
fire and water.
Yet He led us out
into refreshment.

65:13 I
will enter into Your house
with burnt offerings.
I will pay my promises
to You,
65:14 which
my lips specified
and my mouth spoke
during my trouble.
65:15 I
will offer burnt offerings
of marrow to You,
with incense.

I will offer rams to You,
oxen with male goats.

65:16 Come, hear,
and I will tell –
all you who fear God –
how much He has done
for my soul!
65:17 I cried out to Him
with my mouth.
I lifted *Him* up
under my tongue.
65:18 If I considered
betrayal in my heart,
the Lord might not hear.
65:19 For this reason,
God heard.
He paid attention
to my petitions' voice.

65:20 God is blessed,
who has removed
neither my prayer
nor His mercy
from me.

Psalm 66:1 (KJV Ps 67)
To *the* end, in hymns,
a psalm of songs.

66:2 May God
be kind to us and bless us.
May He light up His face
over us, and be kind to us,
66:3 so we may know
Your way in *the* land –
Your security among
all nations.
66:4 May peoples
confess to You, God.
May all peoples confess
to You.
66:5 May nations
be happy and exult,
because You judge
peoples in equity.
You direct nations
in *the* land.
66:6 May peoples
confess to You, *O* God.
May all peoples confess
to You.

66:7 *The* land
has given its fruit.
May God bless us, our God.
66:8 May God bless us.
May all land's ends
fear Him.

Psalm 67:1 (KJV Ps 68)
To *the* end, by David,
a psalm of song.

67:2 May God rise up.
May His enemies
be scattered and flee –
those who have hated Him
to His face.
67:3 May they vanish
like smoke vanishes.
As wax melts
before fire's face,
so may sinners perish
before God's face.
67:4 Yet may *the* fair feast.
May they exult in God's sight.
May they delight in happiness.

67:5 Sing to God!
Chant *a* psalm in His name!
Make *a* way to Him
who climbs up
over *the* sunset!
The Lord *is* His name.
Rejoice in His sight!
May they be troubled
by His face.
67:6 *He is*
the orphans' father,
the widows' judge –
God in His holy *place*.
67:7 God makes one type
to live in *a* house –
God, who leads
the defeated out in strength,
just as much as
those who frustrate,
those who live in tombs.

67:8 God,
when You went out
in Your people's sight,
when You crossed over
in *the* desert,
67:9 *the* land moved,
the skies dropped down –
before *the* face
of Sinai's God,
before *the* face
of Israel's God.

67:10 You
set aside rain *as a* gift,
O God, to Your inheritance,
It is weakened.
Truly, You perfected them.
67:11 Your animals live in it.
You planned for *the* poor one
in sweetness, *O* God.
67:12 *The* Lord
will give *the* Word
to those telling good news,
with great force.
67:13 *The* King of strength
is of *the* chosen,
of *the* chosen.
The splendor of *the* house
is to divide spoils.
67:14 so that you may sleep
in *the* midst of lots,
of doves' wings

stripped of silver,
the end parts of its back,
in gold's paleness.
67:15 When he sees
the heavenly One,
You will rule over them.
They will be whitened
more than snow in Selmon[45].

67:16 God's mountain
is a fat mountain,
a congealed mountain,
a fat mountain,
67:17 as you would suspect,
congealed mountains,[46]
a mountain in which
God was pleased to dwell,
for *the* Lord will live
in *the* end.

67:18 God's chariots
are ten thousand,
many thousands, rejoicing.
The Lord *is*
among them in Sinai,
in *the* holy place.
67:19 You ascended
into *the* highest.
You captured captivity.
You received gifts
among men,
for even non-believers
to inhabit *the* Lord,
O God.

67:20 *The* Lord *is* blessed
daily, every day.
He will make *a* way
prosperous to us,
God of our security.
67:21 God, our God,
is making secure.
Death's exit belongs
to *the* Lord, *the* Lord.
67:22 Even so,
God will shatter
His enemies' heads,
the hairy *heads* of those
walking around in their
crimes.

67:23 *The* Lord spoke,
"I will turn back from
Bashan[47].
I will turn back
into *the* deepest seas,
67:24 "so your foot
may be plunged in blood,
your dog's tongue *satisfied*
from your enemies
themselves."

67:25 They will see

---

[45] Mount Selmon is first mentioned in scripture at Judges 9:48.

[46] These are images of great abundance, in the thought-world of the psalmist.

[47] Bashan is first mentioned in scripture at Numbers 21:23.

Your way, *O* God,
my God, my King's way,
who is in *the* holy *place*.
67:26 Princes
have gone before,
singing psalms together –
among young women,
playing instruments.

67:27 In *the* gatherings,
bless God,
the Lord of Israel's fountains!
67:28 There
is Benjamin *the* youth,
in his mind's zeal,
Judah's princes, their leaders,
Zebulon's princes,
Nepthali's princes.

67:29 Command
Your strength, God!
Strengthen this, God!
What You have done is for us.
67:30 From
Your temple in Jerusalem,
kings will bring gifts to You.
67:31 Rebuke
the wild *beasts of the* reeds,
the bulls' gathering
among *the* people's cows,
that they may set apart
those who have been proved
like silver!
Scatter nations who want war!
67:32 They will send
a representative from Egypt.

Ethiopia stretches out
its hand before God.

67:33 Sing
to God, O land's rulers!
Chant psalms to *the* Lord!
Chant psalms to God,
67:34 who climbs up
over *the* sky's sky,
to *the* east!
Look, He will sound
His voice, strength's voice.

67:35 Give glory to God!
His magnificence
is over Israel.
His strength *is* in *the* clouds.
67:36 God's wonders
are among His holy ones.
Israel's God Himself
will give strength and courage
to His people.

God *is* blessed.

Psalm 68:1 (KJV Ps 69)
To *the* end,
for those
who will be changed,
of David.

68:2 Make me secure, God,
for waters have reached
even up to my soul!
68:3 I am stuck
in *a* profound mess
There is no substance.
I have come
to *the* sea's depths.
A storm sunk me.
68:4 I labored, crying out.
My throat has become hoarse.
My eyes failed
while I hope in my God.
68:5 Those who hated me
without cause are multiplied
more than my head's hairs.
Those who persecuted me
are strengthened –
those who are
my enemies unfairly.
What I did not take away,
I then had to pay back.

68:6 God,
You know my foolishness.
My offenses against You
aren't hidden.
68:7 May those
who wait for You,
Lord, not be ashamed of me.

Strength's Lord,
may those who seek You
not be dismayed
on my account.

Israel's God,
68:8 on Your behalf
I suffered reproach.
Confusion covered my face.
68:9 I became *a* stranger
to my brothers,
a homeless wanderer
to my mother's children,
68:10 because zeal
for Your house consumed me.
The reproaches of those
reproaching You fell on me.

68:11 I buried
my soul in fasting,
and this has become
a criticism against me.
68:12 I put on
repentance's clothing,
and became *a* joke to them.
68:13 Those who
sat in *the* gate
practiced against me.
Those who drank wine
sang songs about me.

68:13 I, truly,
direct my prayer
to You, *O* Lord,
asking for a time
of good will, God,

in Your mercy's multitude.
Hear me,
in Your security's truth!
68:15 Pull me
out of *the* mud,
that I not be caught tight!
Let me be freed
from those who hate me –
from deepest waters.
68:16 May *the* storm
not submerge me in water,
nor swallow me in *the* depths.
Nor may *a* well close
its mouth over me.

68:17 Hear me, Lord,
for Your mercy is kind!
According to Your
compassion's multitude,
look at me!
68:18 Do not
turn Your face away
from Your servant,
for I am troubled!
Hear me quickly!
68:19 Understand
my soul and free it!
Rescue me because
of my enemies!

68:20 You know
my insult and confusion –
my reverence.
68:21 All who
trouble me are in Your sight.
My heart expected insult
and misery.
At *the* same time,
I sustained one
who might share my sadness,
yet he did not come –
one who might console,
yet I did not find *him*.

68:22 They
gave me gall for my food.
In my thirst they gave me
vinegar.
68:23 May their table
be made *a* trap before them,
in revenges and in scandal.
68:24 May their eyes
be obscured,
nor may they see.
May their back
always be bent down.
68:25 Pour
Your anger out over them!
Let Your wrath's fury
catch up to them!
68:26 May their dwelling
become desert.
May there be no one
who lives in their tents.
68:27 For one
whom You struck,
they have persecuted.
They added to my wounds'
pain.

68:28 Pile up betrayal
over their betrayal,

that they may not enter
into Your fairness!
68:29 May they be erased
from *the* living's book,
and not be written down
with *the* fair.

68:30 I am
a poor, hurting man.
Your security, God,
supported me.
68:31 I will
praise God's name with song.
I will lift Him up in praise.
68:32 *It* will be
more pleasing to God
than *a* young calf –
than bringing forth horns
and hooves.

68:33 May *the* poor
see and be happy.
Seek God and Your soul
will live!
68:34 For *the* Lord
heard *the* poor.
God has not despised
His prisoners.

68:35 May skies
and earth praise Him –
sea and everything
creeping in them.
68:36 For God
will make Sion secure.
Judah's cities will be built,
They will live there
and will acquire it
by inheritance.
68:37 His slaves' seed
will possess it.
Those who delight
in His name
will live in it.

Psalm 69:1 (KJV Ps 70)
To *the* end, of David,
in memory of One
who made me safe –
the Lord.

69:2 God,
exert *Yourself* on my behalf!
Lord, hurry to help me!
69:3 May they be
dismayed and awe-struck
who hunt my soul.
69:4 Let them
be turned back and ashamed
who want harm for me.
Let them be
turned aside, ashamed,
who say about me,
"Good! Good!"

69:5 Let them rejoice
and be happy in You –
all who seek You.
May they always say,
"God be glorified,"
who love Your security.

69:6 I, truly,
am needy and poor.
God, help me!
You are my helper
and my liberator, Lord.
Don't delay!

Psalm 70:1 (KJV Ps 71)
David, *a* psalm of Jonadab's[48]
children, and those who were
formerly captives.

I have hoped in You, Lord.
May I not be dismayed
in eternity.
70:2 In Your fairness,
free me and rescue me!
Turn Your ear toward me
and make me safe!
70:3 Be for me
God *the* protector –
a fortified place --
that You may make me
secure!
You are my foundation
and my refuge.

70:4 My God, rescue me
from sinners' hands,
from *the* hands of those
working against *the* law,
and *from the* treacherous,
70:5 because You are
my patience, Lord –
my hope from my youth,
Lord!
70:6 I have been
strengthened in You
from *the* uterus,
from my mother's womb.

---

[48] Jonadab's story begins in 2 Samuel 13.

You are my protector.
My song *is* always in You.
70:7 I have become
like *a* wonder to many.
You *are a* mighty helper.
70:8 May my mouth
be filled with praise,
that I may sing
Your glory all day –
Your greatness.

70:9 Do not cast me away
in old age's season,
when my strength fails!
Do not abandon me,
70:10 for my enemies
have spoken against me!
Those who guarded my soul
took counsel as one,
70:11 saying,
"God has abandoned him.
Attack and take him,
because *there* is no one
to rescue!"

70:12 God,
do not withdraw from me!
My God, look down
and help me!
70:13 May they be
dismayed and disappointed
who are dragging
my soul away.
May those who seek my harm
be covered in confusion
and shame.

70:14 But I will always hope,
and add over all Your praise.
70:15 My mouth
will announce Your fairness
all day – Your security –
for I have not known
literature.[49]
70:16 I will enter
in *the* Lord's power.
Lord, I will be mindful
only of Your fairness.

70:17 God,
You have taught me
from my youth
even to *the* present.
I will tell Your wonders.
70:18 Even in old age
and infirmity, *O* God,
do not abandon me,
until I have told
Your might to all
the generation which
is coming – Your power!

70:19 Your fairness, God,
is even in *the* highest.
What great things
You have made, God!
Who is like You?
70:20 How many great
and harmful troubles

---

[49] He has no other voice than his own with which to praise God. Literature would follow.

You have shown me!
Again, You have
given me life,
and led me back again
from *the* land's depths.
70:21 You have
multiplied our greatness.
Again, You are
my consolation.
70:22 For now I will confess
Your truth to You
in vessels of psalms, *O* God.
I will sing to You on guitar,
Israel's Holy *One*.
70:23 My lips will rejoice
when I have sung to You –
my soul, which You
bought back.
70:24 And my tongue also
will meditate all day
on Your fairness –
when those who sought
my harm were confused
and turned back.

Psalm 71:1 (KJV Ps 72) In
Solomon.

71:2 God,
give *the* King Your judgment,
the King's son Your fairness –
to judge Your people
in fairness,
Your poor in judgment!
71:3 May mountains support
the people's peace,
and hills *their* fairness.

71:4 He will judge *the* poor
among *the* people,
and make *the* poor's
children secure.
God will humiliate
those who abuse *them.*
71:5 He will endure
with *the* sun
and before *the* moon,
generations of generations.
71:6 *God* will come down
like rain in fleece,
like rain drops falling gently
over *the* land.
71:7 Fairness will arise
in His days,
peace's abundance,
until *the* moon
is taken away.

71:8 He will rule
from sea even to sea,
from *the* river

even to *the* ends
of *the* land's circle.
71:9 Ethiopians will fall
prostrate before Him,
and His enemies
will lick *the* dust.
71:10 Kings
of Tharsis and islands
will bring gifts.
Kings of Arabia and Saba
will bring presents.
71:11 All kings
will adore Him.
All nations will serve Him,
71:12 because He freed
the poor from *the* powerful –
the poor who had no helper.
71:13 He will spare
the poor and powerless.
God will make
the poor's souls secure.
71:14 He will buy back
their souls from usury
and betrayal.
Their name *will be* valued
before Him.

71:15 He will live.
It will be given to Him
from Arabia's gold.
71:16 *There* will be
a foundation in *the* land,
in *the* mountains' heights.
His fruit will be raised up
over Lebanon,
From *the* city

they will flourish
like *the* land's grass.

71:17 May His name
be blessed in ages.
May His name endure
before *the* sun.
All *the* land's tribes
will be blessed in Him.
All nations will bless Him.

71:18 *The* Lord God
is blessed – Israel's God,
who alone works wonders.
71:19 Blessed *is* His
majesty's name in eternity!
May all *the* land be filled
by His majesty.

May it be!

May it be!

71:20 *The* praises
of David, son of Jesse,
have ended.

End of Book Two

Book Three

Psalm 72:1 (KJV Ps 73)
A psalm of Asaph.

How good God is to Israel,
to those who are upright
in heart!
72:2 But for me, *my* feet
were almost moved.
My steps were
almost poured out,
72:3 because I was jealous
of *the* treacherous,
seeing sinners' peace.
72:4 For *there* is no
consideration of their death,
or firmness in their wound.
72:5 They are not
in men's labor,
and they will not
be beaten with men.
72:6 Therefore,
pride had them.
They are covered
by their treachery
and lawlessness.
72:7 Their treachery
will ooze out like fat.
They passed away
in heart's affection.

72:8 They thought
and spoke in worthlessness.
They spoke betrayal
in *the* highest.
72:9 They placed
their mouth in *the* sky.
Their tongue has passed
through *the* land.

72:10 Therefore, my people
will be turned back here,
and full days will be found
among them.
72:11 They will say,
"How does God know?
Is *there* even knowledge
in *the* Most High?"

72:12 Look, they are sinners.
Yet, prospering in *the* age,
they have obtained riches.
72:13 I said, therefore,
"I have made my heart right,
and washed my hands
among *the* innocent,
for no reason."

72:14 I was beaten all day.
My punishment *came*
in *the* morning.
72:15 If I said,
"I will speak this way,"
look, I have condemned
Your children's nation.
72:16 I supposed I knew.
This is hard work before me.
72:17 Until I enter
into God's sanctuary,
I will understand

about their end.

72:18 Nevertheless,
You appointed them
because of lies–
You threw them down
while they were lifted up.
72:19 How they are made
into desolation!
They were destroyed
suddenly.
They died because
of their treachery.
72:20 Like *a* dream
to one waking up, Lord,
You will reduce their image
to nothing in Your city.

72:21 For
my heart was inflamed
and my insides were changed.
72:22 I was
reduced to nothing
and I did not know
72:23 that I have become
like *a* beast of burden
with You.
I *am* always with You.

72:24 You held
my right hand.
You led me out in Your will,
and sustained me with glory.
72:25 For what
is mine in *the* sky,
apart from You?
What have I desired on earth?
72:26 My flesh
has come to nothing
and my heart *as well*,
O my heart's God.
My portion *is* God in eternity.
72:27 For look, *those* who
keep themselves
far from You will die.
You have destroyed
all who prostitute themselves,
far from You.

72:28 *It is* good
for me, though, to stick
to God.
It is good to put my hope
in *the* Lord God,
so I can announce
all Your messages
in Sion's daughter's gates.

Psalm 73:1 (KJV Ps 74)
Understanding of Asaph.[50]

Why, God,
have *You* driven *us* back
to *the* end?
Your fury was aroused
over Your pasture's sheep.
73:2 Remember
Your assemblies,
what You have possessed
from *the* beginning!
You bought back
Your inheritance's rod –
Mount Sion,
which You have inhabited.
73:3 Lift up Your hands
over their pride in *the* end!
How harmful is *the* enemy
in *the* holy place!

73:4 Those who hated You
were glorified in *the* midst
of Your observances.
They hung banners –
their banners,
73:5 and they
did not consider.
As if in crossing
over *a* summit,
as if in *a* wooded forest,
by axes

73:6 they
destroyed His gates
in *the* thing itself.
With hatchets
and carpenters' axes,
they destroyed them.
73:7 They burned
Your sanctuary in *the* land
with fire.
They violated Your name's
dwelling *place*.
73:8 They said
in their heart –
all their blood kin together –
"Let us make
all God's feast days silent
in *the* land."

73:9 We
have not seen our signs.
Already there is no prophet.
He will not know us further.
73:10 How long, God,
will *the* enemy enter in?
Does Your name's adversary
provoke to *the* end?
73:11 Why do You turn
back Your hand,
and Your right hand
from *the* middle
of Your chest to *the* end?

73:12 But God
was our King before *the* age.
He worked prosperities
in *the* land's midst.

---

[50] This Psalm commemorates the destruction of Solomon's Temple in Jerusalem by the Babylonians, 587 B.C.E.

73:13 You strengthened *the* sea in Your strength. You crushed *the* dragons' heads in *the* waters.
73:14 You crushed *the* dragon's skull. You gave him *as* meat to Ethiopia's people.
73:15 You disrupted springs and torrents. You dried up Etham's rivers.

73:16 Day is Yours. Night is Yours. You made dawn and sun.
73:17 You made all *the* land's ends. Summer and spring-time – You fashioned them.

73:18 Remember these! *The* enemy rushed in at *the* Lord. Foolish people aroused His name.
73:19 Do not hand *the* soul trusting You over to beasts! Do not forget *the* souls of Your poor to *the* end!
73:20 Regard Your covenant, because those who are *the* land's forgotten are filled up by treacherous houses!

73:21 May *the* humble not be turned back *or* made confused. *The* poor and *the* powerless will praise Your name.
73:22 Rise up, God! Judge Your cause! Remember Your insults, from those who live from foolishness all day!
73:23 Do not forget Your enemies' voices! *The* pride of those who hated You rises up always.

Psalm 74:1 (KJV Ps 75)
To *the* end
that you may not corrupt.
A psalm of Asaph,
in song.

74:2 We will
confess to You, God.
We will confess
and invoke Your name.
We will tell Your wonders.
74:3 When I
will have grasped *the* time,
I will judge justices.

74:4 *The* land melted,
and all who live in it.
I have strengthened
its columns.
74:5 I said
to *the* treacherous,
"Do not work betrayal!"
and to those falling short,
"Do not exalt strength!"
74:6 "Do not praise
your strength in conceit!
Do not speak treachery
against God,
74:7 "neither from *the* east,
nor from *the* west,
nor from desert mountains!

74:8 "For God is judge.
He humiliates this *one*
and lifts this *one* up.
74:9 *A* chalice
full of unmixed wine
is stirred up
in *the* Lord's hand.
He has poured *it* out
from this to that,
yet no dregs are drained.
All *the* land's sinners
will drink.

74:10 But I
will proclaim in *the* age.
I will sing to Jacob's God.
74:11 I will smash
all sinners' strengths,
but *the* strengths of *the* fair
will be lifted up.

Psalm 75:1 (KJV Ps 76)
To *the* end, in praises,
a Psalm of Asaph,
a song to Assyria.[51]

75:2 God *is* known in Judah.
His name *is* great in Israel.
75:3 His place
was made in peace.
His dwelling *is* in Sion.
75:4 There He
has broken powers –
bow, shield, sword, and war.
75:5 You
shine forth amazingly
from eternal mountains.

75:6 All
the mindless are troubled.
They slept their sleep
in heart.
All men found nothing
from their hands' riches.
75:7 At your rebuke,
Jacob's God,
they slept who rode up
on horseback.
75:8 You are terrifying.
Who will resist You?
Your wrath *remains*
from that time

75:9 You have made
Your judgment heard
from *the* sky.
The land feared and fell silent
75:10 when You rose up
in judgment, *O* God,
to make *the* land's
gentle *ones* secure.
75:11 For men's thoughts
will confess to You.
Reflection's remnant
observes *a* feast day to You.

75:12 Promise and pay
to *the* Lord your God –
all who *are* around Him!
Bring gifts to
the Terrifying One –
75:13 to Him who takes away
the breath of terrifying rulers,
among *the* land's kings!

---

[51] Assyria was the ancient superpower that destroyed the northern kingdom of Israel in 722 B.C.E. The story of Assyria's interaction with Israel begins in 2 Kings 15:19.

Psalm 76:1 (KJV Ps 77)
To *the* end, for Idithun,
a psalm of Asaph.

76:2 By my voice
to *the* Lord –
I cried out
by my voice to God,
and He understood me.
76:3 In my trouble's day,
I searched for God,
with my hands lifted up
to Him at night.
I was not deceived.
My soul refused
to be consoled.
76:4 I remembered God
and was delighted.
I have worked hard
and my spirit
was disappointed.
76:5 My eyes
anticipated wakeful vigils.
I was troubled
and have not spoken.
76:6 I thought
about ancient days.
In my mind I had
eternal years.
76:7 I meditated
by night in my heart.
I exercised
and sought my spirit.

76:8 Will God
cast aside in eternity
and not bring near –
that *it* may be more pleasing
up to now?
76:9 Or, will He take
His mercy away
in *the* end –
from generation
to generation?
76:10 Or, will God
forget to have mercy,
or hide His mercies
in His anger?

76:11 I said,
"Now I have begun.
This *is the* change
of *the* Most High's
right hand."

76:12 I was mindful of
the Lord's works,
for I will remember
Your wonders
from *the* beginning.
76:13 I will meditate
on all Your works.
I will practice
in all Your inventions.

76:14 *O* God, Your way
remains in *the* holy.
Who *is a* great god
like our God?
76:15 You are God,
who work wonders.

You made Your strength
known among peoples.
76:15 You bought back
Your people by Your arm –
Jacob and Joseph's children.

76:16 *The* waters
saw You, God.
The waters saw You
and were afraid.
The abysses were stirred up.
76:18 *The* multitude
of *the* water's sounds
gave *their* voice,
for Your arrows passed
through *the* clouds.

76:19 Your thunder's voice,
whirling around,
illuminated *the* land's circles
by Your flashes.
The land moved and trembled.
76:20 Your way *is* in *the* sea,
Your paths in many waters.
Your footsteps will not
be known.
76:21 You led
Your people out like sheep,
by Moses' and Aaron's hand.

Psalm 77:1 (KJV Ps 78)
Understanding of Asaph.

Listen to My law, my people!
Incline your ear
to My mouth's words!
77:2 I will
open my mouth in parables.
I will speak propositions
from *the* beginning,

77:3 How much
we have heard!
We have known them
and our fathers have told us.
77:4 They were not hidden
from their children
in another generation –
telling *the* Lord's praises
and His strengths,
His wonders,
which He worked.
77:5 He stirred up
testimony in Jacob
and placed *a* law in Israel –
as much as He commanded
our fathers –
to make it known
to their children,
77:6 that
another generation may know,
children who will be born
and rise up,
and will tell it
to their children;
77:7 that they may place

their hope in God,
not forget God's works,
and seek His commandments.
77:8 May they not be
like their fathers,
a twisted and exasperating
generation,
a generation which
did not direct its heart!
Its spirit has not trusted God.

77:9 Ephraim's children,
stretching and shooting
the bow,
were turned back
in *the* day of war.
77:10 They did not keep
God's covenant,
and did not want
to walk in His law.
77:11 They
forgot His blessings
and His wonders,
which He showed them
77:12 before their fathers,
wonders which He worked
in Egypt's land,
in Tanis's field.[52]

77:13 He divided *the* sea
and led them through.
He stood waters
as if *in a* wine skin.
77:14 He led them out

---

[52] See Numbers 13:22.

in *a* cloud by day
and in fire's illumination
all night.
77:15 He broke open *a* rock
in *the* wasteland
and gave them water,
as if from *the* great abyss.
77:16 He brought water
from *a* rock,
and led *it* out
like rivers of waters.

77:17 Yet they
were disposed to that point
to sin against Him.
They provoked *the* Most High
in anger in *a* waterless *desert*.
77:18 They tempted God
in their hearts,
that they might beg food
for their desires.
77:19 They spoke
dismissively of God.
They said, "God can't prepare
a table in *the* desert, can He?
77:20 "Even though
He struck *a* rock
and waters flowed out,
and they flooded in torrents,
He can't give bread
or prepare *a* table
for His people, can He?"

77:21 Therefore, *the* Lord
heard and dismayed them.
Fire was kindled in Jacob.

Wrath rose up in Israel,
77:22 because they did not
believe in God
or hope in His security.
77:23 He commanded
from *the* clouds above
and opened *the* sky's doors.
77:24 He rained on them
manna to eat
and gave them
the sky's bread.
77:25 Man
ate *the* angels' bread.
He sent them food
in abundance.

77:26 He took away
the south wind from *the* sky,
and led *the* southwest wind
in His strength.
77:27 He rained over them
meat like dust,
feathered birds
like *the* sea's sand.
77:28 They fell
in *the* middle of their camp,
around their tents.
77:29 They ate
and were filled to excess.
He brought their desire
to them.
77:30 They were not
cheated of their desire
until their food was
in their mouth.

77:31 God's wrath
rose over them.
He killed their fat ones,
and blocked Israel's chosen.
77:32 Through all these,
they continued sinning,
and did not trust His wonders.
77:33 Their days
ended in futility,
their years with haste.

77:34 When He killed them,
they sought Him
and turned back.
They came to God early.
77:35 They were reminded
that God is their helper.
God Most High their
redeemer.
77:36 They loved Him
with their mouth,
yet their tongues lied to Him.
77:37 But their heart
was not honest with Him,
nor did they have faith
in His covenant.

77:38 But He is merciful
and will make atonement
for their sins,
He will not destroy them.
He was bountiful,
that He might turn
His anger aside,
and not ignite all His anger.
77:39 He remembered

that they are flesh,
a breath that goes
and does not return.

77:40 How often they
angered Him in *the* desert!
They enraged Him
in wrath in *the* wasteland.
77:41 They turned back
and tempted God.
They enraged
Israel's Holy One.
77:42 They did not
remember His hand,
the day in which
He bought them back
from *the* troubling hand,
77:43 even as He appointed
His signs in Egypt,
His wonders in Tanis's field.

77:44 He turned
their river into blood
and their *rain* showers,
so they could not drink.
77:45 He sent
biting flies among them
and consumed them,
and frogs, and scattered them.
77:46 He gave
their fruit to blight,
their hard work to locusts.
77:47 He killed
their vines with hail,
their fruit trees with frost.

77:48 He handed
their beasts over to hail,
and their possessions to fire.
77:49 He sent among them
His indignation's wrath –
anger and ingrafted trouble,
sent in by harmful angels.
77:50 He made
a way for His anger's path.
He did not spare
their souls from death.
He closed up
their cattle in death.
77:51 He struck all
the first born in Egypt's land,
their hard work's first fruits
in Ham's tents.[53]

77:52 He took
His people out like sheep,
and led them in *the* desert
like *a* flock.
77:53 He led them
out in hope.
They did not fear.
He buried their enemies
in *the* sea.
77:54 He led them
to His holiness's mountain,
which His right hand
had acquired.
He threw nations out

---

[53] Ham, one of Noah's sons, was the ancestor of the Egyptians. His story begins in Genesis 5:32.

from before their face
and divided *the* land
by lot for them,
in distribution's cord.
77:55 He made
Israel's tribes live in their
tents.

77:56 Yet they tempted
and angered God Most High,
and did not keep
His testimonies.
77:57 They turned
themselves back,
and did not serve
the covenant,
just like their fathers
turned back
into *a* twisted stronghold.
77:58 In anger,
they stirred Him up
in their hills.
They provoked Him
to jealousy
by their sculpted images.

77:59 God heard and scorned
and vigorously drove Israel
back to nothing.
77:60 He rejected

Shiloh's[54] tent – His tent,
where He lived among men.
77:61 He handed
their strength over
to captivity,
their beauty to *the* enemy's
hand.
77:62 He shut
His people up by *the* sword
and spurned His inheritance.
77:63 Fire consumed
their young men.
Their young women
were not mourned.
77:64 Their priests
fell by *the* sword,
and their widows
will not weep.

77:65 *The* Lord
woke up, as if sleeping,
like *a* mighty one,
drunk with wine.
77:66 He struck
His enemies in pursuit.
He gave them lasting shame.
77:67 He rejected
Joseph's tent
and did not choose
Ephraim's tribe.
77:68 He chose Judah's tribe,

---

[54] Shiloh's first mention in scripture is in Genesis 49:10. Its story as the place of the Lord's tent of meeting begins in Joshua 18.

Mount Sion, which He loved.
77:69 He built up
His holiness like *a* unicorn,
in *the* land which He founded
in *the* age.
77:70 He chose
David, His slave,
and took Him from
flocks of sheep,
from following birthing ewes.
He accepted him
77:71 to pastor
Jacob, His slave,
and Israel, His inheritance.
77:72 He fed them
in his heart's innocence,
and led them out
in his hands' understanding.

Psalm 78:1 (KJV Ps 79)
A psalm of Asaph.

Nations have come
into Your inheritance.
They have polluted
Your holy temple.
They have made Jerusalem
into *a* storehouse for fruit.
78:2 They left *the* dead
among Your servants
as food for *the* sky's birds –
Your holy ones' flesh
for *the* land's beasts.
78:3 They poured out
their blood like water
around Jerusalem.
There was no one
who buried *them*.
78:4 We became
our neighbors' ridicule,
mockery and scoffing
to those who live around us.

78:5 How long, Lord?
Will You be wrathful
to *the* end?
Will Your jealousy
blaze up like fire?
78:6 Pour out Your anger
in nations which
have not known You,
in kingdoms which
have not invoked Your name,
78:7 who consumed Jacob
and desolated his place!

78:8 Do not remember
our ancient betrayal!
Let Your mercies
go quickly before us,
because we are have been
made poor beyond measure!
78:9 Help us,
God of our security,
for *the* sake
of Your name's glory!
O Lord, free us!
Be our sins' atonement,
for Your name's sake!
78:10 Unless, perhaps,
they say among *the* nations,
"Where is their God?"
May *the* vengeance
of Your slaves' blood,
which is poured out,
be made conspicuous
before our eyes!

78:11 May *the* groan
of shackled *exiles*
enter into Your sight!
According to
Your arm's greatness,
possess *the* destroyed ones'
children!
78:12 Repay into
our neighbors' breasts
seven times over their taunt,
with which they insulted You,
Lord!

78:13 But Your people –
Your pasture's sheep –
we will confess You
in *the* age.
We will announce Your praise
in generation after generation.

Psalm 79:1 (KJV Ps 80)
To *the* end,
testimony for those
who will be changed,
a psalm of Asaph.

79:2 *You* who
rule Israel, understand!
You who lead Joseph
out like sheep,
who sit above cherubim,
make Yourself known!
79:3 Before Ephraim,
Benjamin, and Manasseh,
show Your power!
Come and make us secure!
79:4 God, convert us!
Show Your face
and we will be secure!

79:5 Lord, God of strength,
how long will You be angry
over Your slave's prayer?
79:6 You fed us
weeping's bread.
You watered us
with tears, in measure.
79:7 You placed us
in contradiction
to our neighbors.
Our enemies mocked us.
79:8 God of strength,
convert us!
Show Your face
and we will be secure!

79:9 You took
a vine out of Egypt.
You cast out nations
and planted her.
79:10 You were
the journey's leader
in her sight.
You planted her roots.
She filled *the* land.
79:11 Her shadow
covered mountains.
Her bushes
were God's cedars.
79:12 She stretched out
her young vines
even to *the* sea,
her seedlings
even to *the* River.

79:13 So, why have You
destroyed her wall?
All who go past *the* way
gather her grapes.
79:14 They
exterminated her.
A woodland pig
and each wild beast
has eaten her.

79:15 God
of strength, turn back!
Look down from *the* sky!
See and visit this vine!
79:16 Perfect her
whom Your right hand
planted,

over *the* child whom
You strengthened for
Yourself!

79:17 Scorched by fire,
undermined by
Your face's rebuke,
they will perish.
79:18 Let Your hand be over
Your right-hand man,
over *the* Son of Man,
whom You strengthened
for Yourself,
79:19 and we
will not withdraw from You.
You will revive us,
and we will invoke
Your name.

79:20 Lord,
God of armies, convert us!
Show Your face,
and we will be secure!

Psalm 80:1 (KJV Ps 81)
To *the* end,
for *the* winepresses,
of Asaph.

80:2 Exult to God our helper!
Shout for joy to Jacob's God!
80:3 Lift up *a* psalm
and play *the* tympani,
the pleasant psalter
with guitar!
80:4 Sound *a* trumpet
at *the* new moon as a sign,
on *the* day of our solemn rites,
80:5 for *it*
is *a* precept in Israel,
and *a* judgment
of Jacob's God!

80:6 He placed it
as testimony in Joseph
when he escaped
Egypt's land.
He heard *a* tongue
which he had not known.
80:7 *God* turned away
burdens from his back.
Israel's hands
had slaved in baskets.

80:8 "In distress
you invoked Me.
I freed you and heard you
in *the* storm's hidden place.
I tested you

at *the* water of contradiction[55].
80:9 "Hear, my people!
I will answer you, Israel,
if you will hear Me.
80:10 "*There* will be
no recent god among you,
nor will you adore
a strange god.
80:11 "For I am
the Lord your God,
who led you from Egypt's
land.
Open your mouth wide
and I will fill it!

80:12 "Yet my people
did not listen to My voice.
Israel did not hear Me.
80:13 "I sent them away
according to their
hearts' desires.
They will walk
in their own inventions.
80:14 "If My people
had heard me,
if Israel had walked
in My ways,
80:15 "perhaps I would have
humiliated their enemies
for nothing.
I would have raised My hand
over those troubling them."

80:16 *The* Lord's enemies
have lied to Him.
Their time will be in *the* age.
80:17 He gave them food
from *the* fat of *the* grain.
He filled them
with honey from *the* rock.

---

[55] See Exodus 17:1-7.

Psalm 81:1 (KJV Ps 82)
A psalm of Asaph.

God stood
in *the* gods' gathering.
God gives judgment
in *their* midst.
81:2 "How long will you
be judged treacherous,
and lift up sinners' faces?
81:3 "Judge *the* needy,
the lowly orphan!
Justify *the* poor!
81:4 "Rescue *the* poor!
Free *the* needy from
sinners' hands!

81:5 They have not known
or understood.
They walk in shadows.
All *the* land's foundations
will be moved.

81:6 "I said, 'You are gods,
all *the* Most High's children.'
81:7 "But you will
die like men.
You will fall like one
of *the* princes"

81:8 Rise up, God!
Judge *the* land,
for You will inherit
among all nations!

Psalm 82:1 (KJV Ps 83) *A* psalm song, of Asaph.

82:2 God,
who will be like You?
Do not be silent
or restrained, God,
82:3 because, look,
Your enemies have shouted!
Those who hated You
raised *their* head.
82:4 They have
maligned counsel
over Your people,
and plotted against
Your holy ones.
82:5 They said, "Come!
Let us ruin them as *a* nation!
Let Israel's name
be remembered no more!"

82:6 For they plotted as one,
together against You.
They made *a* pact –
82:7 *the* Edomites'
and Ishmaelites tents,
Moab and *the* Aggarenes,
82:8 Gebal,
Ammon, and Amalek,
foreign nations,
with Tyre's inhabitants.
82:9 For even Assyria
comes with them.
They have become
Lot's children's allies.

82:10 Make them
like Midian[56] and Sisera,
like Jabin in *the* Kison
River[57]!
82:11 They were
destroyed in Endor.
They became like
the land's dung.
82:12 Make their princes
like Oreb and Zeeb,[58]
like Zebah and Zalmunah,[59]
all their princes,
82:13 who said,
"Let us possess
God's sanctuary
by inheritance."

82:14 My God,
make them like *a* wheel,
like stubble before
the wind's face!
82:15 As fire
which burns *a* forest,
as flames burning mountains.
82:16 so You will pursue
them in Your storm.
You will trouble them
in Your anger.

82:17 Fill
their faces with shame,
and they will seek Your name,
Lord!
82:18 May they be
ashamed and troubled
in *the* age of ages!
May they be dismayed
and perish!

82:19 They will know
that Your name *is the* Lord.
You alone are Most High
in all *the* land.

---

[56] For Midian, see Numbers 31:3ff.

[57] For Sisera and Jabin, see Judges 4:2ff.

[58] See Judges 7:25.

[59] See Judges 8:5ff.

Psalm 83:1 (KJV Ps 84)
To *the* end,
for *the* winepresses,
a psalm of Korah's sons.

83:2 How delightful
are Your tents,
O Lord of armies!
83:3 My soul desires
and has fallen short
in *the* Lord's courtyards.
My heart and my flesh
exulted in *the* living God.
83:4 For even *a* sparrow
found itself *a* home,
a dove her nest,
where she places her chicks –
at Your altars,
Lord of armies,
my King and My God.

83:5 Those who live
in Your house *are* blessed.
In ages of ages
they will praise You!
83:6 Blessed is man,
whose help *is* from You.
God[60] has arranged progress
in his heart,
83:7 in *the* valley of tears,
in *the* place which he set up.

83:8 For even *the* Lawgiver
will give blessings.
They will go
from strength to strength.
The gods' God
will be seen in Sion.

83:9 Lord God of armies,
hear my prayer!
Jacob's God,
perceive with *Your* ears!
83:10 God, our protector,
look on and consider,
in Your Christ's face!
83:11 For one day
in Your courtyards
is better than
a thousand *elsewhere*.
I have chosen to be nothing
in my God's house,
rather than to live
in sinners' tents.

83:12 For God delights
in mercy and truth.
The Lord will give
grace and glory.
83:13 He will not
deprive of good those
who walk in innocence.
Lord of armies,
man who hopes in You
is blessed.

---

[60] Literally, "He."

Psalm 84:1 (KJV Ps 85)
To *the* end,
a psalm of Korah's sons.

84:2 You blessed
Your land, Lord.
You turned aside
Jacob's captivity.
84:3 You paid back
Your people's treacheries.
You covered all their sins.
84:4 You lessened
all Your anger.
You turned away from
Your indignation's wrath.
84:5 Convert us,
our security's God!
Turn Your anger
away from us!

84:6 Will You be angry
with us in eternity,
or extend Your anger
from generation to
generation?
84:7 God, You, turning,
will revive us.
Your people will rejoice
in You.
84:8 Show us, Lord,
Your mercy!
Give us Your security!

84:9 May I hear
what *the* Lord God
says in me –
for He will speak peace
among His people –
over His holy ones,
and among those
who will be converted
from *the* heart.
84:10 Even so,
those fearing Him
are near His security,
that glory may dwell
in our land.

84:11 Mercy and truth
will meet each other.
Fairness and peace
have kissed.
84:12 Truth
has risen from *the* land.
Fairness looked down
from *the* sky.
84:13 For *the* Lord
will give even kindness.
The land will give its fruit.
84:14 Fairness
will walk before Him.
He will place their steps
in *the* way.

Psalm 85:1 (KJV Ps 86)
A prayer
of David himself.

Incline Your ear, Lord,
and hear me,
because I am
poor and weak!
85:2 Guard my soul,
because I am holy!
Make Your slave safe,
hoping in You, my God!
85:3 Have
mercy on me, Lord,
for I will cry out to You
all day!

85:4 Make
Your slave's soul happy,
for I lifted up my soul
to You, Lord!
85:5 For you, Lord,
are soft and gentle,
of many mercies
to those who invoke You.

85:6 Perceive my prayer
with *the* ear, Lord!
Understand my prayers'
voice!
85:7 In trouble's day
I called out to You,
because You have heard me.

85:8 No one is like You
among gods, Lord.
There is no one
according to Your works.
85:9 All nations which You
have made will come
and worship before You,
Lord,
and will glorify Your name,
85:10 for You are great,
working wonders.
You alone are God.

85:11 Lead me out,
Lord, in Your way,
and I will go forward
in Your truth!
May my heart be happy,
that it may fear Your name.
85:12 I will confess to You,
Lord my God, in all my heart.
I will glorify Your name
in eternity,
85:13 for Your mercy
is great over me.
You rescued my soul
from *the* lower inferno.

85:14 God, betrayers
have risen up against me.
A mighty gathering
sought my soul.
They have not placed You
in their consideration.
85:15 You, Lord God,
are compassionate
and merciful, patient,
of great kindnesses,

and truthful.
85:16 Look on me
and have mercy on me!
Give Your rule
to Your helper!
Make Your slave-woman's
son secure!
85:17 Work for me
a sign, in goodness!
Let those who hated me
see and be dismayed,
for You, Lord, helped me.
You consoled me.

Psalm 86:1 (KJV Ps 87)
A psalm of song,
of Korah's sons

Its foundations
are in holy mountains.
86:2 *The* Lord delights
in Sion's gates,
more than all Jacob's tents.
86:3 Glories
are spoken of you, God's City.

86:4 "I will be mindful
of Rahab[61] and Babylon,
of those who know me.
Look – foreign nations
and Tyre
and *the* Ethiopian people –
these were there."
86:5 Won't Sion say,
'*This* man and *that* man
were born in her'?
He established her,
the Most High.
86:6 *The* Lord will tell
of peoples and princes
in writings,
of those who were in her.
86:7 Residence in you
is like *the* rejoicing of all.

---

[61] Rahab's story begins in Joshua 2.

Psalm 87:1 (KJV Ps 88)
A psalm song,
of Korah's sons,
to *the* end, for Maheleth,
understanding to respond,
Eman *the* Ezrahite.

87:2 Lord,
God of my security,
day and night I cried out
before You.
87:3 Let my prayer
enter into Your sight!
Incline Your ear to my plea,
87:4 because my soul
is full of harms!
My life has drawn
near *the* inferno.
87:5 I am considered
with those going down
into *the* pit.
I have become
like *a* man without help,
87:6 free among *the* dead,
like *the* killed
sleeping in their graves,
of whom You have
no further memory.
They are cast out
of Your hand.
87:7 They put me
in *the* lower pit, in darkness,
in death's shadow.

87:8 Your fury is
strengthened over me.
All Your floods
have washed over me.
87:9 You have made
my acquaintances
stay far away from me.
They considered me
an abomination to themselves.
I was handed over
and did not come out.
87:10 My eyes
fainted from poverty.
I called to You, Lord, all day.
I held out my hands to You.

87:11 You won't work
miracles for *the* dead,
will you?
Will *the* healed rise up
and confess to You?
87:12 Will someone tell
Your mercy in *the* grave,
or Your truth in destruction?
87:13 Will Your wonders
be known in darkness,
or Your fairness
in oblivion's land?

87:14 I myself
have cried out to you, Lord.
My prayer will come before
You early.
87:15 Yet why, Lord,
do You turn my prayer back?
You turn Your face
away from me.

87:16 I am poor,
working hard since my youth,
lifted up, yet I am
humiliated and troubled.
87:17 Your rages
passed through me.
Your terrors troubled me.
87:18 They surrounded me
like water all day.
They encircled me at once.

87:19 You alienated
friend and neighbor from me,
those I know,
because of suffering.

Psalm 88:1 (KJV Ps 89)
Understanding,
of Ethan *the* Ezrahite.[62]

88:2 I will sing
the Lord's mercies in eternity.
In generation after generation,
I will tell Your truth
with my mouth,
88:3 for You
have spoken in eternity.
"Mercy will be built
in *the* skies."
Your truth will be
prepared in them.
88:4 "I
have arranged *a* covenant
with my chosen *ones*.
I have sworn to David
my slave.
88:5 "Even in eternity
I will prepare your seed.
I will build your throne
in generation
after generation."

88:6 They will confess
Your wonders to *the* sky,
Lord, for Your truth *lives*
in *the* holy *ones'* gathering.

---

[62] This psalm recites the covenant God made with David, then recounts before God the shattered state of David's throne following the exile. Notice, despite the psalmist's almost reproachful tone toward God, the emphatic, unexpected ending.

88:7 For who in *the* clouds
is equal to *the* Lord?
Who will be like *the* Lord
among God's children –
88:8 God, who is glorified
in *the* holy ones' council,
great and awesome
over all who are
around Him?
88:9 Lord God of armies,
who is like You?
You are mighty, Lord.
Your truth *is* around You.

88:10 You master
the sea by power.
You calm its moving waves.
88:11 You humiliated
the proud like *the* slaughtered.
You scattered Your enemies
by Your arm's strength.
88:12 Skies are Yours
and *the* land is Yours.
You established
the land's circles
and its bounty.
88:13 You created
north wind and sea.
Tabor and Hermon
will exult in Your name.
88:14 Your arm
moves with power.
May Your hand
be strengthened –
Your right hand *be* lifted up.
88:15 Fairness and judgment
are Your throne's preparation.
Mercy and truth
go before Your face.

88:16 *The* people
who knows jubilation
is blessed, Lord.
They will walk
in Your face's light.
88:17 They will exult
in Your name all day.
They will be lifted up
in Your fairness.
88:18 For You are
their strength's glory.
In Your good pleasure,
our power will be
lifted up.
88:19 For our assumption
is of *the* Lord,
and of Israel's Holy One,
our King.

88:20 Then You
spoke in *a* vision
to Your holy *ones,* and said,
"I put *My* help
in *the* mighty *one*.
I lifted up *the* chosen
from My people.
88:21 "I found
David, My slave.
I anointed him in holy oil.
88:22 "For My hand
will help him.
My arm will strengthen him.

88:23 *"An* enemy
will accomplish nothing
against him.
A traitorous son
will not set harm
before him.
88:24 "I will cut down
his enemies before his face.
I will turn those who hate him
to flight.
88:25 "My truth
and my mercy *will be*
with him.
In My name his strength
will be exalted.
88:26 "I will place
his hand on *the* sea,
his right hand on rivers.
88:27 "He will invoke me:
'You are my Father –
my God –
my security's sustainer.'
88:28 "I will place him first,
most high before *the* land's
kings.
88:29 "I will watch over
My mercy toward him
in eternity,
and my covenant
by faithfulness to him.
88:30 "I will place his seed
in *the* age of ages,
his throne like *the* sky's days.

88:31 "If his children
fall away from My law,
and cease to walk
in My judgments,
88:32 "if they
profane my fairness
and fail to keep
my commandments,
88:33 "I will visit
their betrayals with *a* rod,
and their sins in beatings.
88:34 "But I will not
scatter My mercy
away from him,
or harm in My truth.
88:35 "Nor will
I profane my covenant.
What proceeds from my lips
I will not make void.

88:36 "I have
sworn once in My holiness.
Will I lie to David?
88:37 "His seed
will endure in eternity.
88:38 "His throne *is*
like *the* sun in My sight,
like *the* moon –
perfect in eternity,
faithful witness in *the* sky."

88:39 Yet You have
rejected and despised.
You put off Your Christ.
88:40 You turned
your slave's covenant
upside down.
You profaned his sanctuary

in *the* land.
88:41 You destroyed
all his borders.
You used his foundation
as *an* object of dread.
88:42 All those passing by
have torn him apart.
He became his neighbor's
curse.

88:43 You lifted up
the right hand of those
harming him.
You made all his enemies
happy.
88:44 You turned away
his sword's help.
You were not his ally in war.
88:45 You destroyed
him from cleanness.[63]
You crushed his throne
in *the* land.
88:46 You reduced
his season's days.
You poured confusion
over him.

88:47 How long, Lord?
Are You turning away
to *the* end?
Will Your wrath
blaze up like fire?
88:48 Remember what
my substance is!
Didn't You make
all men's children fleeting?
88:49 Who is *the* man
who will live
and not see death?
Will he rescue
his *own* soul
from *a* dead hand?

88:50 Where are
Your ancient mercies, Lord,
as You swore to David
in Your truth?
88:51 Be mindful, Lord,
of Your slaves' shame,
which I have shut up in my
chest from many nations –
88:52 what Your enemies
cursed, Lord –
what they cursed
in exchange for Your Christ!

88:53 *The* Lord *is* blessed
in eternity.

May it be.

May it be.

---

[63] The Temple's destruction brought to an end Israel's sacrificial system and, with it, its ability to make ritual atonement for sin.

End of Book Three

Book Four

Psalm 89:1 (KJV Ps 90)
A prayer of Moses,
God's man.

Lord, You have been
a refuge to us
in generation
after generation.
89:2   Before
mountains were made
or land and worlds
were formed,
from age even to age
You are God.
89:3   Do not
turn man back in humiliation!

You said, "Turn back,
men's children!"
89:4   For *a* thousand years
before Your eyes
are like yesterday
which has passed,
and *a* night's watch.
89:5   What they esteem
for nothing,
so their years will be.

89:6   Early, like grass,
he may pass through.
Early he may flower
and pass through.
At evening, he may wilt,
harden, and dry up.

89:7   For we
are weakened in Your anger.
We are troubled in Your fury.

89:8   You placed
our treacheries in Your sight,
our age in Your face's light.
89:9   For all our days
have perished in Your anger.
Our years failed.
They were considered
like *a* spider's web.
89:10   Our years' days
in themselves are seventy
years, or perhaps,
in strength, eighty –
full of hard work and pain,
for weakness comes upon *us*
and we will be swept away.

89:11   Who has known
Your anger's power –
before Your fear, Your anger
89:12   to consider?
So make Your right *hand*
known, and *we*,
shackled in heart,
will live in wisdom.
89:13   Turn again, Lord!
How long?
Be open to Your
slaves' prayers!

89:14   We were
filled early by Your mercy.
We exulted and delighted

in all our days.
89:15 We were
happy for *the* days
in which You humbled us,
years in which we saw harm.

89:16 Look on Your slaves!
In Your works
guide even their children!
89:17 May *the* Lord
our God's splendor be
over us!
Guide our hands works
above us!
Direct our hands' work!

Psalm 90:1 (KJV Ps 91)
A praise song, of David.

One who lives
in *the* Most High's help,
will dwell
in *the* sky's God's protection.
90:2 He will say to *the* Lord,
"You are my sustainer
and my refuge, my God.
I will hope in Him,
90:3 "for He will free me
from *the* hunter's trap,
from *the* sharpened word."

90:4 On His shoulders
He will defend you,
and you will hope
under His wings.
90:5 His truth, like a shield,
will surround you.
You will not fear
the night's dread,
90:6 *the* arrow
flying in *the* day,
the trouble stalking
in shadows,
the invasion
and *the* noon-day demon.

90:7 *A* thousand
will fall at your side –
ten thousand
at your right hand –
yet it will not come
close to you.

90:8 Even so, you will
consider with your eyes.
You will see
sinners' retribution.

90:9 For You, Lord,
are my hope.
You have made
the Most High your refuge.
90:10 Harms will not
be added to you.
Beating will not
come near your tent.
90:11 For He will command
His angels concerning you,
that they keep you
in all your ways.
90:12 They will
carry you by hand,
lest perhaps you strike
your foot against *a* stone.

90:13 You will walk
over asps and basilisks.
You will trample
lion and dragon.[64]
90:14 "For he
has hoped in me,
and I will free him.
I will protect him
because he has known
My name.
90:15 "He will
cry out to me,
and I will hear him.
I am with him in trouble.
I will rescue him
and make him famous.
90:16 "I will fill him
with length of days.
I will show him
My security."

---

[64] Note the progression from physical to figurative in this verse's parallels.

Psalm 91:1 (KJV Ps 92)
A psalm of song,
in *the* Sabbath day.

91:2 *It* is good
to confess to *the* Lord,
and to sing to Your name,
Most High –
91:3 to make Your mercies
known in *the* morning,
Your truth at night –
91:4 on *a* ten-stringed harp,
with *a* song on guitar –
91:5 because You
delighted me, Lord,
in Your creation.
I will rejoice
in Your hands' work.
91:6 How great
are Your works, Lord!
Your thoughts have become
exceedingly profound.

91:7 Dull man
will not recognize.
A fool will not
understand this –
91:8 when sinners
are cut down like grass –
all who work betrayal –
so they can be destroyed
in *the* age of ages.

91:9 But You
are Most High in eternity,
O Lord.

91:10 For look,
Your enemies, Lord!
For look, Your enemies
will die and be scattered –
all who work betrayal.

91:11 My strength will be
lifted up like *a* unicorn.
My old age *will be lifted up*
into *a* nourishing mercy.
91:12 My eye
looked down on my enemies,
those rising up against me.
My ear will hear
those planning harm.

91:13 *The* fair,
like *a* palm tree, will flourish.
He will be multiplied
like Lebanon's cedars.
91:14 Planted
in *the* Lord's house,
they will flourish
in our God's courtyards.
91:15 They
will be multiplied still
into *a* nourishing old age.
The suffering *ones*
will be well,
91:16 so they can tell
that *the* Lord our God is right.
There is no betrayal in Him.

Psalm 92:1
A praise song, of David,
on *the* day before *the* Sabbath,
when *the* land was inhabited.

The Lord has reigned.
He is clothed in beauty.
The Lord is clothed
in strength.
He encircled Himself,
for He established
the land's circle,
which will not be moved –
92:2 prepared *as* Your throne
from that time.
You exist from *the* age.

92:3 *The* rivers
lifted up, *O* Lord.
The rivers lifted up
their voice.
The rivers lifted up
their floods –
92:4 from
many waters*'* voices.
The sea's ecstasies
are wonderful.
The Lord *is* wonderful
in *the* highest.

92:5 Your testimonies
have been made
overwhelmingly convincing.
Holiness befits Your house,
Lord, in length of days.

Psalm 93:1 (KJV Ps 94)
Psalm of David,
for *the* fourth Sabbath.

The Lord *is* revenge's God,
Revenge's God has acted
openly.
93:2 Be lifted up,
You who judge *the* land!
Return vengeance
to *the* proud!

93:3 How long
will sinners, Lord –
how long will sinners
be glorified?
93:4 They
will declare solemnly
and speak betrayal.
All who work unfairly
will speak.

93:5 Your people, Lord
were humiliated.
Your inheritance
was shocked.
93:6 Widow and stranger
were destroyed.
Orphans were killed.
93:7 They said,
"*The* Lord will not see.
Jacob's God will not
understand."

93:8 Understand,
you who are dull

among *the* people!
Fools, at long last, be wise!
93:9 Does One
who planted *the* ear not hear,
or One who molded *the* eye
not consider?
93:10 Does One who
reproaches nations not prove?
Does One who teaches men
not understand?
93:11 *The* Lord knows
man's thoughts,
that they are pointless.

93:12 Blessed is *a* man
whom You will teach, Lord,
whom, from Your law,
You will instruct,
93:13 so You can soothe him
through harmful days,
until he may dig
the sinner's grave.
93:14 For *the* Lord will not
push His people away.
He will not abandon
His inheritance
93:15 until fairness
is returned to judgment,
and all whose hearts are right
are beside her.

93:13 Who
will stand up with me
against *the* malignant,
or who will stand with me
against those working
treachery?
93:17 If *the* Lord
had helped me *a* little less,
my soul would have dwelled
in *the* inferno.
93:18 If I said,
'My foot is moved,'
Your mercy, Lord, helped me.

93:19 According to *the*
multitude of my heart's pain,
Your consolations
made my soul happy.
93:20 Could
inequality's seat be near You,
You who shape suffering
into teaching?
93:21 They will hunt
a fair one's soul.
They will condemn
innocent blood.
93:22 Yet *the*
Lord has become
a refuge for me –
my God, my hope's helper.

93:23 He will repay
their treachery to them.
He will ruin them
in their *own* malice.
The Lord our God
will ruin them.

Psalm 94:1 (KJV Ps 95)
A praise song, of David.

Come, let us rejoice
in *the* Lord!
Let us sing joyfully
to our security's God!
94:2 Let us seize
upon His face in confession!
Let us sing joyfully to Him
in psalms,
94:3 for *the* Lord
is a great God,
a mighty King over all gods,
94:4 for *the* land's ends
are in His hand!
Mountains' heights are His.
94:5 *The* sea is His.
He made it.
His hands have formed
dry *land*.

94:6 Come, let us adore
and fall prostrate!
Let us weep before *the* Lord
who made us!
94:7 For He is our God
and we *are* people
of His pasture,
sheep of His hand.

94:8 "Today
if you hear His voice,
do not harden your hearts,
94:9 "as in *the* provocation,
according to testing's day
in *the* desert,
where your fathers tested Me.
They tested Me and saw
My works.
94:10 "Forty years I was
offended by that generation.
I said, 'They always
wander away in heart.'
94:11 "They did not
understand My ways,
so that I swore in my anger
whether they will enter into
my peace."

Psalm 95:1 (KJV Ps 96)
When *the* house was built,
after captivity, *a* song to
David.

Sing to *the* Lord
a new song!
Sing to *the* Lord,
all *the* land!
95:2 Sing to *the* Lord!
Bless His name!
Announce His security
from day to day!
95:3 Announce His glory
among nations,
His wonders in all peoples!
95:4 For *the* Lord is great,
supremely worth of praise.
He is terrifying over all gods.
95:5 For all
the nations' gods are demons,
but, truly, *the* Lord made
the skies.

95:6 Confession and beauty
are in His sight.
Holiness and magnificence
are in His holiness.
95:7 Bring to *the* Lord,
fathers of nations,
bring glory and honor
to *the* Lord!
95:8 Bring *the* Lord
His name's glory!
Lift up sacrifices
and enter into His courts!

95:9 Adore *the* Lord
in His holy court!
May all *the* land
be moved by His face.
95:10 Say among nations
that *the* Lord reigns!
For He even
has set right *the* world,
that it not be moved.
He will judge peoples
in fairness.

95:11 Let skies be happy
and land rejoice.
Let sea and its plenty
be moved.
95:12 Fields will rejoice,
and all that are in them.
Then *the* forest's every tree
will be joyful
95:13 before *the* Lord's face,
for He is coming
to judge *the* land.
He will judge *the* land's circle
in fairness,
and peoples in His truth.

Psalm 96:1 (KJV Ps 97)
To David, when his land was restored.

The Lord reigned.
Let *the* land exult!
Let *the* many islands
be joyful!
96:2 Clouds and gloom
are around Him.
Fairness and judgment
are His throne's correction.
96:3 Fire precedes Him.
It will burn His enemies
around.
96:4 His flashes
enlightened *the* land's circle.
The land saw and was moved.
96:5 Mountains
melted like wax
before *the* Lord's face,
before *the* face
of *the* land's Lord.
96:6 Skies
announced His fairness.
All peoples saw His glory.

96:7 May all
who adore statues,
who glory in their images,
be dismayed.
Adore Him, all His angels!

96:8 Sion
heard and was happy.
Judah's daughters exulted
because of Your judgments,
Lord.
96:9 For You are
the Most High Lord
over all *the* land.
You are overwhelmingly
exalted over all gods

96:10 You who delight
in *the* Lord, hate harm!
He keeps His saints' souls.
He will free them
from sinners' hands.
96:11 Rising light
is to *the* fair,
and joy to *the* upright heart.
96:12 Be joyful
in *the* Lord, fair ones!
Confess His sanctification's
memory!

Psalm 97:1 (KJV Ps 98)
A psalm of David.

Sing to *the* Lord a new song,
for He has worked wonders!
His right hand has saved
by itself, His holy arm.
97:2 *The* Lord has made
His security known
in *the* nations' sight.
He has revealed His fairness.
97:3 His
mercy is remembered
and His truth to Israel's house.
All *the* land's ends
have seen our God's security.

97:4 Sing
joyfully to *the* Lord,
all *the* land!
Sing and exult
and offer psalms!
97:5 Sing
psalms to *the* Lord on guitar,
on guitar with *the* voice
of psalm!
97:6 With metal trumpets
and *the* cornets' voice,
sing joyfully in *the* sight
of *the* king's Lord!

97:7 Let sea
and its bounty be moved,
land's circles and those
who live in them.
97:8 Rivers applaud by hand.
Mountains will exult together
97:9 in *the* Lord's sight,
for He comes to judge
the land.
He will judge land's circle
in fairness,
and peoples in equity.

Psalm 98:1 (KJV Ps 99)
A psalm of David.

The Lord has reigned.
Let peoples be angry!
There is One who sits
over *the* cherubim.
The land is moved.
98:2 *The* Lord
is great in Sion.
He is most high
over all peoples.
98:3 Let them confess
Your name's greatness,
for *it* is terrible and holy.

98:4 *The* King's honor
delights in judgment.
You have prepared
right living.
You made judgment
and fairness in Jacob.
98:5 Lift up *the* Lord our God
and adore his feet's
footstool,[65] for *it* is holy.

98:6 Moses and Aaron
are among His priests.
Samuel *is* among those
who invoke His name.
They invoked *the* Lord
and He heard them.
98:7 He spoke to them
in *a* column of cloud.[66]
They kept His testimony
and *the* precept He gave them.

98:8 Lord our God,
You heard them.
God, You were satisfaction
to them,[67]
punishing all their inventions.

98:9 Lift up
the Lord our God!
Worship in His holy
mountain,
because *the* Lord our God
is holy!

---

[65] Isaiah 66:1 Thus says the LORD: "Heaven is my throne and the earth is my footstool; what is the house which you would build for me, and what is the place of my rest? (RSV)

[66] See Exodus 13:21.

[67] God makes atonement on their behalf, offering Himself as the victim.

Psalm 99:1 (KJV Ps 100)
A psalm in confession.

99:2 Sing joyfully
to *the* Lord, all *the* land!
Serve *the* Lord in happiness!
Enter into His sight
in exultation!
99:3 Know
that *the* Lord – He is God!
He made us,
and not we ourselves.
We are His people,
sheep of His pasture.
99:4 Enter His gates
in confession,
His courts in hymns!
Confess to Him!
Praise His name,
99:5 because
the Lord is pleasing!
His mercy *lives* in eternity,
His truth even in generation
after generation.

Psalm 100:1 (KJV Ps 101)
A psalm of David.

I will sing
mercy and judgment.
I will sing psalms
to You, Lord,
100:2 that I may understand
in *a* unstained way.
When You come to me,
I will walk
in my heart's innocence,
in my house's midst.
100:3 I did not place
an unfair cause
before my eyes.
I hated those
working deceptions.
Such a one did not stay
close to me.

100:4 *A* twisted heart
turns away from me.
I did not think spitefully.
100:5 I pursued
those insulting their
neighbor secretly.
A proud eye
and *a* greedy heart –
with such I did not eat.
100:6 My eye *remained*
with *the* land's faithful ones,
so they could sit with me.
One walking in *a* spotless
path served me.
100:7 One who

works pride did not live
in my house's midst.
One who tells betrayal
did not govern
in my eyes' sight.
100:8 In *the* morning,
I killed all *the* land's sinners –
so I could destroy
all who work treachery
from *the* Lord's city.

Psalm 101:1 (KJV Ps 102)
A poor man's prayer, when he
was anxious, and he poured
out his plea before *the* Lord.

101:2 Lord, hear my prayer!
May my cry come to You.
101:3 Do not
turn Your face away from me!
In whatever day
I am troubled,
turn Your ear toward me!
In whatever day I invoke You,
hear me quickly!

101:4 For my days have
passed away like smoke.
My bones have dried up
like *a* womb.
101:5 It was struck like hay.
My heart dried up,
so that I have forgotten
to eat my bread.
101:6 From
my moaning's voice,
my bones stuck fast
to my flesh.
101:7 I became
like *a* pelican in solitude.
I became like *a* raven
on *a* house.
101:8 I kept watch.
I became like *a* single sparrow
on *a* roof.

101:9 All day my enemies

rebuked me.
The ones who praised me
swore against me,
101:10 for I have
eaten ashes like bread.
I mixed my cup with tears
101:11 from Your anger
and indignation's face –
because, *in* lifting *me* up,
You crushed me.
101:12 My days
declined like *a* shadow.
I dried up like grass.

101:13 But you, Lord,
endure in eternity.
Your memorial *remains*
in generation
after generation.
101:14 You, rising up,
will have mercy on Sion,
because *it* is time
to have mercy –
because *the* time comes.
101:15 For its stones
have pleased Your servants,
and its lands will receive
mercy.
101:16 Nations will fear
the Lord's name,
and all *the* land's kings
Your glory.
101:17 For *the* Lord
will build Sion,
and it will be seen
in His glory.

101:18 He respected
a humble *one's* prayer,
and has not spurned their plea.

101:19 Let this be written
in another generation.
People who will be born
will praise *the* Lord,
101:20 because
the Lord looked down
from His holy place's height .
He considered land from sky,
101:21 so He could hear
the shackled peoples' cry –
so He could free
the destroyed ones' children –
101:22 so He could announce
the Lord's name in Sion –
His praise in Jerusalem;
101:23 in gathering
peoples as one – and kings –
that they might serve *the* Lord.
101:24 He answered him
in His strength's path.

Warn me about
the briefness of my days!
101:25 Do not call me back
in *the* middle of my days!
Your years *endure*
in generation after generation.
101:26 At *the* beginning,
You, Lord, founded *the* land.
The skies *are* Your hands'
work.
101:27 They will perish,

but You endure.
All *those*, like clothing,
will wear out.
You will change them
like *a* blanket,
and they will be changed.

101:28 But You,
Lord, are *the* same.
Your years will not fail.
101:29 Your
slaves' children will live.
Their seed will be guided
in *the* age.

Psalm 102:1 (KJV Ps 103)
Of David himself.

Bless *the* Lord, my soul,
and all that is in me
bless His holy name!
102:2 Bless
the Lord, my soul,
and do not forget
all His retributions –
102:3 who makes atonement
for all Your treacheries,
who heals all your infirmities,
102:4 who
buys back your life
from destruction,
who crowns you in mercy
and compassions,
102:5 who
fills your desire in good!
Your youth will be renewed
like *an* eagle's –
102:6 *the* Lord,
working mercies,
and judgment to all
who suffer harm.

102:7 He has made
His ways known to Moses,
His purposes to Israel's
children.
102:8 *The* Lord
is compassionate
and merciful,
patient and greatly merciful.
102:9 He

will not be angry forever,
or threaten in eternity.
102:10 He has not worked
with us according to our sins,
or repaid us according
to our injustices,
102:11 for, according to
sky's distance from land,
He has strengthened
His mercy over those
who fear Him.
102:12 As far as sunrise
stands from sunset,
He has made our treacheries
far from us.
102:13 *The* same way
a father has mercy
on children,
the Lord is merciful
to those who fear Him

102:14 For He
has known our unreality.
He remembered
that we are dust.
102:15 Man's days
are like grass.
Like *a* field's flower,
so he will blossom.
102:16 For *the* wind
has blown through him
and he will not stand.
His place will know him
no further.

102:17 But *the* Lord's mercy *remains* from eternity,
even in eternity,
over those who fear Him.
His fairness *remains*
to children's children,
102:18 to those
who serve His covenant
and remember
His commandments,
to do them.
102:19 *The* Lord
has prepared His throne
in *the* sky.
His reign will rule all.

102:20 Bless
the Lord, His angels,
mighty *ones* in strength,
working His word,
to *the* hearing
of His commandments' voice!
102:21 Bless *the* Lord,
all His armies,
His ministers,
who work His will!
102:22 Bless
the Lord, all His works,
in every place
of His domain!

Bless *the* Lord, my soul!

Psalm 103:1 (KJV Ps 104)
Of David himself.

Bless *the* Lord, my soul!

Lord my God,
You are greatly lifted up.
You have put on confession
and beauty,
103:2 cloaked
in light like clothing,
extending sky like *a* tent;
103:3 who covers
His heights in waters;
who makes
cloud His stairway;
who walks
on *the* winds' wings;
103:4 who makes
Your angels winds,
Your ministers burning fire;
103:5 who founded *the* land
over its bases.
It will not be bent down
in *the* age of ages.
103:6 *The* abyss,
like clothing, *is* its cloak.
Waters will stand
over mountains.

103:7 At Your rebuke
they will flee.
At Your thunder's voice,
they will fear.
103:8 Mountains
will climb up
and fields climb down,
to *the* place
which You established
for them.
103:9 You placed
a boundary which they may
not cross,
nor may they turn back
to cover *the* land –
103:10 *You*, who send out
springs in valleys.
Waters will pass through
between mountains.
103:11 All
the field's beasts will drink.
The wild donkeys will wait
in their thirst.
103:12 Sky's birds
will live over them.
They will give their cry
from *the* rocks' midst.

103:13 Watering mountains
from their heights,
the land will be satisfied
with Your works' fruit –
103:14 producing
grass for cattle,
herb for men's slaves,
that You may bring out bread
from *the* earth.
103:15 Wine makes
man's heart happy,
that *his* face
may be gladdened by oil,

and his heart may be
strengthened by bread.
103:16 *The* field's trees
will be satisfied,
and Lebanon's cedars,
which You have planted.
103:17 There sparrows
will build nests.
The heron's house
is their leader.
103:18 *The* highest
mountains *are given*
to *the* deer,
rocks of refuge to hedgehogs.

103:19 He made
the moon in *its* seasons.
Sun has known its setting.
103:20 You
appointed darkness
and night was made.
All *the* forest's animals
pass through in it –
103:21 young lions roaring,
that they may capture *prey*.
They seek meat for
themselves from God.
103:22 Sun rises
and they gather together.
They will lie down
in their dens.
103:23 Man
will go out to his work,
to his dealings,
even to evening.

103:24 How magnificent
are Your works, Lord!
You have made all
in wisdom.
The land is filled
by Your possession.
103:25 This *is the* great sea
and its spacious hands.
There are reptiles
beyond number,
small animals with large.
103:26 There ships will pass.
That *is the* dragon,
which You formed
to play in it.

103:27 All wait for You,
that You may give them
food in season.
103:28 When
You give it to them,
they will gather it.
Opening Your hand,
all will be filled
with goodness.
103:29 But,
turning away You face,
they will be troubled.
You will take away
their breath
and they will die.
They will be turned back
into their dust.
103:30 You will
send out Your breath
and they will be created.

You will renew
the land's face.

103:31 May
glory be to *the* Lord
in *the* age!
The Lord
will be happy
in His works –
103:32 who
looks upon *the* land
and makes it tremble;
who touches mountains
and they smoke.

103:33 I will sing to *the* Lord
throughout my life.
I will sing psalms
to my God as long as I am.
103:34 May my words
be pleasing to Him.
I, truly, will delight
in *the* Lord.
103:35 May sinners
be destroyed from *the* land
and betrayers thus will not be!

Bless *the* Lord, my soul!

Psalm 104:1 (KJV Ps 105)
Alleluia.
Confess to *the* Lord
and invoke His name!
Tell His works
among nations!
104:2 Sing to Him!
Sing psalms to Him!
Tell all His wonders!
104:3 Give praise
in His holy name!
Let *the* heart
of those seeking *the* Lord
be happy.
104:4 Seek *the* Lord
and be strengthened!
Seek His face always!

104:5 Remember
His wonders
who made His amazing *works*,
His mouth's judgments –
104:6 Abraham,
His servant's seed,
Jacob, His chosen's children!
104:7 He
is *the* Lord our God.
His judgments
are in all *the* land.

104:8 He has remembered
His covenant in *the* age,
the words which He
commanded
in *a* thousand generations,
104:9 which He assigned

to Abraham –
His oath to Isaac.

104:10 He established
that *promise* to Jacob
in precept,
to Israel in
an eternal covenant,
104:11 saying to you,
"I will give you Canaan's land
as Your inheritance's line" –
104:12 when they were
few in number,
very small, His aliens.
104:13 They passed through
from nation to nation,
from kingdom to another
people.
104:14 He did not allow
man to harm them.
He rebuked kings
on their behalf.
104:15 "Do
not touch my Christs!
Do not seek harm
among my prophets!"

104:16 He called famine
over *the* land.
He destroyed
all *the* bread's foundation.
104:17 He sent
a man before them.
Joseph was sold as *a* slave.
104:18 His feet
were humiliated
in chains.
Iron passed through his soul,
104:19 until
his word came *true*.
The Lord's word
inflamed him.
104:20 *The* king
sent and freed him.
The peoples' ruler
even released him.
104:21 He made him
lord of his house,
ruler of all his possessions.
104:22 that he might teach
his princes like himself,
and teach his elders prudence.

104:23 Israel
entered into Egypt.
Jacob was *a* neighbor
in Ham's land.[68]
104:24 He greatly
increased His people,
and strengthened them
over His enemies.
104:25 He
changed their heart
so that they hated His people,
so that they worked deceit
among His slaves.
104:26 He sent
Moses, His slave,

---

[68] Ham, one of Noah's sons, was the father of the Egyptians, according to Genesis 10:6.

Aaron, whom He chose
for himself.
104:27 He
placed among them
words of His signs
and wonders in Ham's land.
104:28 He sent shadows
and darkened *the land*.
He did not grieve His words.
104:29 He turned
their waters into blood,
and killed their fish.
104:30 Their land
produced frogs,
even into their kings'
inner rooms.
104:31 He spoke,
and biting flies
and stinging insects
came into all their country.
104:32 He appointed
their rains *as a* hail of fire,
burning in their land.
104:33 He struck
their vines and their fig trees.
He broke their country's trees.
104:34 He spoke,
and locusts and grasshoppers
came, who could not
be numbered.
104:35 They ate
all *the* land's grass.
They ate all *the* land's fruit.
104:36 He struck all
their land's firstborn,
first fruits of all
their hard work.

104:37 He led them out
with silver and gold.
There was not *a* sick *one*
among their tribes.
104:38 Egypt was happy
at their leaving,
because their fear
brooded over them.
104:39 He spread out
a cloud for their protection,
and fire that guided them
by night.
104:40 They asked,
and quail came.
He filled them
with *the* sky's bread.
104:41 He broke open *a* rock
and waters flowed.
Rivers went out
into dry *wasteland*,
104:42 because He
was mindful of His holy word,
which He had for Abraham
His servant.

104:43 He led out
His people in exultation,
His chosen ones
in happiness.
104:44 He gave
them nations' lands.
They possessed *the* peoples'
hard work,
104:45 that they may keep

His reasons and seek His law.

Psalm 105:1 (KJV Ps 106)

Alleluia.
Confess to *the* Lord,
for He *is* good,
for His mercy
endures in *the* age!
105:2 Who will speak
powers to *the* Lord?
He will make
all His praises heard.
105:3 Those who will
keep judgment
and work fairness
in every season
are blessed

105:4 Be mindful of us, Lord,
in Your people's well-being!
Visit us in Your health –
105:5 to seeing
Your chosen ones' good,
to rejoicing
in Your nation's happiness!
May You be praised
with Your inheritance.

105:6 We did wrong
with our fathers.
We acted unfairly.
We worked betrayal.
105:7 Our fathers in Egypt
did not understand
Your wonders.
They were not mindful
of Your mercies' multitudes.

They provoked,
coming up to *the* sea,
the Red Sea.
105:8 He made them secure
because of His name –
so He might make
His power known.
105:9 He
rebuked *the* Red Sea
and it was dried up.
He led them in abysses
as in desert.
105:10 He made
them secure from *the* hand
of those who hate.
He bought them back
from *the* enemy's hand.
105:11 Water covered
those troubling them.
Not one remained of them.

105:12 They
believed in His words.
They praised His praise.
105:13 They worked quickly.
They forgot His works.
They did not sustain
His counsel.
105:14 They
desired earthly desires
in *the* desert.
They tempted God
in waterless *wasteland*.
105:15 He
gave them their petition.
He sent satisfaction

into their soul.
105:16 They provoked
Moses in *the* camp –
Aaron, *the* Lord's holy *one*.
105:17 *The* land opened
and swallowed Dathan.
It buried Abiram's
gathering.[69]
105:18 Fire blazed up
in their synagogue.
Flame burned up sinners.

105:19 They
made *a* calf in Horeb.
They adored *the* idol.
105:20 They
changed His glory
into *the* form
of *a* calf, eating grass.
105:21 They forgot God
who made them safe,
who worked mighty *acts*
in Egypt –
105:22 wonders
in Ham's land,
terrors in *the* Red Sea.

105:23 He spoke
that He might destroy them.
If Moses, His chosen one,
had not stood on their side
in His sight,
that He might turn

---

[69] The story of Dathan and Abiram begins in Numbers 16.

His anger away,
He might have
destroyed them.
105:24 They held
the desired land as nothing.
They did not believe
His word.
105:25 They
grumbled in their tents.
They did not listen to
the Lord's voice.
105:26 He lifted up
His hand over them.
How He struck them down
in the desert!
105:27 How He threw
their seed down
among nations,
and scattered them
around regions!

105:28 They
were initated at Baalpeor.
They ate sacrifices
for *the* dead.[70]
105:29 They provoked Him
in their inventions,
and ruin was multiplied
among them.
105:30 Phineas stood up
and made atonement,
and *the* violent shaking
ceased.

105:31 *It* is
reputed to him as fairness
in generation
after generation –
even in eternity.
105:32 They
provoked Him at *the* water
of Contradictions.
Moses was shocked
by them,[71]
105:33 for they
provoked his spirit.
He distinguished in his lips.
105:34 They
did not destroy *the* nations,
as *the* Lord said to them.
105:35 They were
mixed together among nations
and learned their works.
105:36 They
served their idols,
and *it* became *a* scandal
to them.
105:37 They
burned their sons
and their daughters
to demons.
105:38 They poured out
innocent blood –
their sons' blood
and their daughters –
whom they sacrificed

---

[70] See Numbers 25:3ff.

[71] See Exodus 17:1-7.

to Canaan's idols.
The land
was destroyed in blood.
105:39 *It* was contaminated
in their works.
They fornicated
in their inventions.
105:40 The Lord
was furiously angry
against His people.
He detested His inheritance.
105:41 He handed them over
into nations' hands.
Those who hated them
ruled them.
105:42 Their
enemies troubled them.
They were humiliated
under their hands.

105:43 He often freed them,
but they provoked Him
in His counsel.
Their were humiliated
in their treacheries.
105:44 Yet He saw
when they were troubled
and heard their prayer.
105:45 He was mindful
of His covenant,
and was sorry for them,
according to His mercy's
multitude.
105:46 He gave
to them in mercies,
in *the* sight of all
who had captured them.

105:47 Make us
safe, Lord our God,
and gather us from nations,
that we may confess
to Your holy name,
and we may glory
in Your praise!
105:48 Blessed
be the Lord, Israel's God,
from age even into age.
Let all people say,
"May it be, may it be!"

End of Book Four

Book Five

Psalm 106:1 (KJV Ps 107)

Alleluia.
Confess to *the* Lord,
because He *is* good,
because His mercy *endures*
in *the* age!
106:2 Let them speak
who were bought back
by *the* Lord,
whom He redeemed
from *the* enemy's hand.
He gathered them
from regions,
106:3 from *the* sun's rise
to *its* setting,
from *the* north wind
to *the* sea.

106:4 They
wandered in solitude,
in *a* waterless waste.
They did not find *the* way
to *an* inhabited city.
106:5 Hungering
and thirsting,
their soul faltered
within them.
106:6 They
cried out to *the* Lord
when they were troubled,
and He rescued them
from their necessities.
106:7 He led
them in *the* right way,
so that they went
into *an* inhabited city.

106:8 Let them confess
to *the* Lord His mercies,
His wonders
to men's children,
106:9 for He satisfied
the empty soul.
He satisfied
the hungry soul
with good.

106:10 Thirsting in darkness
and bound by death's shadow,
in begging and iron *bonds*,
106:11 because
they provoked God's words,
and exasperated
the Most High's counsel,
106:12 their heart
was humiliated
in their hard work.
They were weak,
nor was there anyone
who would help.
106:13 They
called out to *the* Lord
when they were troubled,
and He freed them
from their necessities.
106:14 He led them
out from darkness
and death's shadow,
and He broke their chains.

106:15 Let His mercies
confess to *the* Lord,
His wonders to men's
children,
106:16 because
He destroyed bronze gates
and shattered iron bars.

106:17 He sustained them
against their treacherous way.
Because of their injustices,
they were humiliated.
106:18 Their soul
despised all food.
They came close
even to death's gates.
106:19 They
cried out to *the* Lord
when they were troubled,
and He freed them
from their necessities.
106:20 He sent His word
and healed them,
and rescued them
from their destroyers.
106:21 Let His mercies
confess to *the* Lord,
His wonders to men's
children.

106:22 Let them sacrifice
an offering of praise.
Let them tell
His works in exultation,
106:23 *those* who go down
to *the* sea in ships,
doing work in many waters.
106:24 They
saw *the* Lord's works,
His wonders in *the* deep.
106:25 He spoke
and *the* gale wind stood.
His floods were lifted up.
106:26 They will climb up
even to *the* skies,
and climb down
even to *the* depths.
Their soul will dissolve
in harms.
106:27 They were troubled.
They staggered like *a* drunk.
All their wisdom
was devoured.
106:28 They
cried out to *the* Lord
when they were troubled,
and He led them out
from their necessities.
106:29 He turned
His storm into *a* breeze,
and His floods grew silent.
106:30 They were happy
because *the floods* were silent.
He led them
into their desire's harbor.

106:31 Let His mercies
confess to *the* Lord,
His wonders to men's
children.
106:32 Let them exalt Him
in *the* people's gathering.

Let them praise Him
in *the* elders' throne.

106:33 He
turned rivers into desert,
waters' outlets into thirst,
106:34 fruitful land
into salty waste,
from *the* ill-will of those
living in it.
106:35 He turned desert
into standing water,
a waterless land
into waters' outlets.
106:36 He
gathered *the* hungry there,
and made them *an* inhabited
city.
106:37 They sowed fields
and planted vineyards.
They bore birth's fruit.
106:38 He blessed them
and they were increased
greatly.
He did not decrease
their cattle.
106:39 They became few.
They shaken
by harms' trouble and by pain.
106:40 Contempt
was poured out over princes.
He made them wander
in *a* trackless *wilderness*,
and not in *the* way.
106:41 He helped
the poor out of poverty
and made families like sheep.

106:42 *The* honest
will see and be happy,
and every treachery
will shut its mouth.
106:42 Who *is* wise
and will keep this?
They will understand
the Lord's mercies.

Psalm 107:1 (KJV Ps 108)
A song of psalms,
of David.

107:2 My heart
is prepared, God.
My heart *is* prepared.
I will sing and chant psalms
in my glory.
107:3 Rise up,
psalter and guitar!
I will rise up early.
107:4 I will confess to You
among *the* peoples, Lord.
I will chant psalms
to You among nations,
107:5 for Your mercy
is great over *the* skies,
Your truth even to *the* clouds.

107:6 Be lifted up
above *the* skies, God,
Your glory over all *the* land –
107:7 so Your
dear *ones* can be freed!
Make secure
by Your right hand,
and hear me!

107:8 God has spoken
in His holy *place*:
"I will lift up
and divide Shechem.
I will measure out
the Valley of Tents.[72]
107:9 "Gilead is mine,
and Manasseh is mine.
Ephraim *is* my head's
undertaking.
Judah *is* my king.[73]
107:10 Moab
is my hope's wash basin.
I will extend my shoe
in Edom.
Foreign nations
have become friends
to me.[74]

107:11 Who will lead me
into *the* fortified city?
Who will lead me
even into Edom?
107:12 Is it not You, God,
who pushed us back?
Will You not go out, God,
with our armies?
107:13 Give us
help from trouble,
because man's security
is useless!

107:14 In God
we will make *an* army.
He will lead our enemies

---

[72] Compare to Vg Ps 59:8.

[73] Compare to Vg Ps 59:9.

[74] Compare to Vg Ps 59:10.

to nothing.

Psalm 108:1 (KJV Ps 109)
To *the* end.
A psalm of David.

108:2 God will not
pass over my praise in silence,
for *a* sinners' mouth,
a liar's mouth,
has opened against me.
108:3 They have spoken
against me by *a* lying tongue,
and surrounded me
by hateful words.
They fought against me
without cause –
108:4 because of this,
that those who favored me
cut me down.
But I prayed.
108:5 They
appointed against me
harm for good,
hatred for my love.

108:6 Put *a* sinner over them!
May *a* devil stand
at their right hands!
108:7 When he is judged,
may condemnation
become visible.
May his prayer
be made into sin.
108:8 May his days
be made few,
and another seize his position.
108:9 May his children

become orphans
and his wife *a* widow.
108:10 Giving way,
may his children
be exiled and beg.
May they be thrown
out of their homes.
108:11 May *a* lender
scrutinize all his wealth.
May foreigners
plunder his hard work.
108:12 May there be
no helper for him,
nor anyone who has pity
on his dependents.
108:13 Let his children
be made for destruction.
In one generation
may his name be forgotten.
108:14 In memory,
let treachery repay his father
in *the* Lord's sight.
May his mother's sin
not be forgotten.
108:15 May they always
be worked against *the* Lord.
May their memory
be destroyed from *the* land,
108:16 for this reason –
because he did not remember
to work mercy.

108:17 He persecuted
the powerless, *the* beggar,
and *the* repentant in heart,
to destroy *them*.

108:18 He
delighted in cursing
and *cursing* will come
to him.
He did not want blessing,
and *blessing* will be far
from him.
He put on cursing
like clothing.
It came into his insides
like water,
into his bones like oil.
108:19 May *cursing*
become for him
like covering clothing,
like *a* girdle which always
clings.

108:20 This *is* their work,
who drag me down
before *the* Lord –
who speak harm
against my soul.
108:21 And you, Lord –
Lord, do for me
according to Your name,
for Your mercy is pleasing!

Free me,
108:22 because
I am needy and poor!
My heart is troubled
within me.
108:23 Like *a* shadow
when it declines,
I am carried away.

I am shaken off like locusts.
108:24 My knees
are weakened from hunger.
My flesh is changed,
because of oil.
108:25 I have become
a reproach to them.
When they saw me,
they shook their heads.

108:26 Help me,
Lord my God!
Make me secure
according to Your mercy!
108:27 Let them know
that this *is* Your hand.
You, Lord, have done this.
108:28 They will curse,
yet You will bless.

May those who rise up
against me be dismayed –
but Your slave will be happy.
108:29 May they
be clothed shamefully
who tear me down.
May they be covered
by their confusion like *a* robe.
108:30 I will
confess exceedingly
to *the* Lord, with my mouth.
I will praise Him
in *the* midst of many,
108:31 because He stood
at *the* poor's right hand,
that He might
make me secure
from those persecuting
my soul.

Psalm 109:1 (KJV Ps 110)
A psalm of David.

The Lord said to my Lord,
"Sit at my right hand,
until I make your enemies
your footstool."
109:2 *The* Lord will send out
your power's rod from Sion,
to rule in His enemies' midst.
109:3 *The* foremost
is with you in *the* day
of your strength,
in *the* holy ones' splendor.
From *the* womb,
before *the* morning star
I birthed you.
109:4 *The* Lord has sworn
and will not repent of it:
"You are priest in eternity,
according to Melchizedek's[75]
order."

109:5 *The* Lord
at your right hand
has broken kings
in His wrath's day.
109:6 He
will judge among nations.
He will fill *them* with corpses.
He will break heads
in *a* populated land.
109:7 He will drink
from *a* torrent in *the* way,
because he will lift up
the Head.

---

[75] See Genesis 14:18.

Psalm 110:1 (KJV Ps 111)
Alleluia.
Of *the* returns of Haggai
and Zechariah.

I will confess to You, Lord,
with all my heart,
in *the* fair ones' council
and gathering.
110:2 *The* Lord's
works are great,
sought out in all His purposes.
110:3 His work *is*
confession and magnificence.
His fairness endures
in *the* age of ages.
110:4 He made
the memory of His wonders.
The Lord *is* merciful
and compassionate.
110:5 He gave food
to those who fear Him.
He will be mindful
of His covenant in *the* age.
110:6 He will tell His people
His works' might,
110:7 that He may give them
nations' inheritance.

Truth and judgment
are His hands' work.
110:8 All His
commandments are faithful,
confirmed in *the* age of ages –
made in truth and equity.
110:9 He sent redemption
to His people.
He commanded
His covenant in eternity.
His name *is* holy
and terrifying.
110:10 Wisdom's beginning
is the fear of *the* Lord,
good understanding
to all doing it.
His praise endures
in age of ages.

Psalm 111:1 (KJV Ps 112)
Alleluia.
Of *the* returns of Haggai
and Zechariah.

A man who fears *the* Lord
is blessed –
one who will desire greatly
in His commandments.
111:2 His seed will be
mighty in *the* land.
An honest generation
will be blessed.
111:3 Fame and riches
will be in his house.
May his fairness endure
in *the* age of ages.
111:4 Light has risen
for *the* honest in darkness –
merciful, compassionate,
and fair.

111:5 *A* man who
has mercy and lends
is pleasing.
He will arrange his words
in judgment,
111:6 because he will not
be moved in eternity.
111:7 *The* fair will be
in eternal memory
He will not fear
on hearing harm.
His heart is ready
to hope in *the* Lord.

111:8 His
heart is established.
He will not be moved,
until he despises his enemies.
111:9 He scattered.
He gave to *the* poor.
May his fairness
endure in *the* age of ages.
His strength will be
lifted up in glory.

111:10 *A* sinner
will see and be angry.
He will grind his teeth,
and melt away.
Sinners' desire will vanish.

Psalm 112:1 (KJV Ps 113)
Alleluia.
Praise *the* Lord, children!
Praise *the* Lord's name!
112:2 May
the Lord's name be blessed,
from this *moment* now
and even in age.
112:3 From *the* sun's rise
even to its setting,
the Lord's name
is worthy of praise.

112:4 *The* Lord is high
above all nations.
His glory *shines* above
the skies.
112:5 Who *is* like
the Lord our God,
who lives in *the* highest?
112:6 He
looks on *the* humble,
in sky and in land,
112:7 rousing *the* powerless
from *the* land,
and lifting *the* poor up
from dung,
112:8 so He can
place him with princes,
with His people's princes,

112:9 *God is the One*
who makes *the* sterile
live in *a* home,
joyful mother of children.

Psalm 113:1 (KJV Ps 114)
Alleluia.
In Israel's exit from Egypt,
Jacob's house
from *a* barbarous people,
113:2 Judah
became His sanctuary,
Israel His power.
113:3 *The* sea saw and fled.
Jordan was turned back.
113:4 Mountains
rejoiced like rams,
hills like *a* flock's lambs.

113:5 What is with you, sea,
that you fled –
and with you, Jordan,
that you were turned back?
113:6 Mountains,
you rejoiced like rams,
and hills, like *a* flock's lambs,
113:7 before *the* Lord's face.
Earth was moved
before *the* face
of Jacob's God,
113:8 who turned *a* rock
into standing water
and *a* cliff
into fountains of water.

113:9 Not to us,
Lord, not to us,
but to Your name give glory –
113:10 because
of Your mercy and Your truth,
unless nations say,

"Where is their God?"

113:11 But our God
is in *the* sky.
All things –
whatever He willed –
He did.

113:12 *The* nations' images
are silver and gold,
a human hand's works.
113:13 They have *a* mouth
but will not speak.
They have eyes,
yet will not see.
113:14 They have ears,
but will not hear.
They have noses,
yet will not smell.
113:15 They have hands,
but will not feel.
They have feet,
yet will not walk.
They will not cry out
in their throat.
113:16 May those
who make them
become like them –
all who trust in them.

113:17 Israel's house
hoped in *the* Lord.
He is their helper
and their protector.
113:18 Aaron's house
hoped in *the* Lord.
He is their helper
and their protector.
113:19 Those
who fear *the* Lord
hoped in *the* Lord.
He is their helper
and their protector.

113:20 *The* Lord was
mindful of us and blessed us.
He has blessed Israel's house.
He has blessed Aaron's house.
113:21 He blessed
all who fear *the* Lord,
small with great.

113:22 May the Lord
add over you, over you
and over your children.
113:23 You
are blessed by *the* Lord,
who made sky and land.
113:24 *The* sky of sky
is to *the* Lord,
but He gave *the* land
to men's children.

113:25 *The* dead will not
praise you, Lord,
nor all who go down
to *the* inferno.
113:26 But we who live –
we bless *the* Lord,
from this *moment* now
and even into age.

Psalm 114:1 (KJV Ps 115)
Alleluia.
I was delighted,
because *the* Lord will hear
my prayer's voice,
114:2 because He inclined
His ear to me.
I will invoke You
in my days.

114:3 Death's pains
surrounded me.
The inferno's dangers
found me.
I found trouble and pain.
114:4 I invoked
the Lord's name.
O Lord, free my soul!
114:5 *The* Lord
is merciful and fair.
Our God has compassion –
114:6 *the* Lord*,*
guarding little ones.
I was humiliated,
and He freed me.

114:7 Turn back, my soul,
to your peace,
because *the* Lord
has done well for you –
114:8 because He rescued
my soul from death,
my eyes from tears,
my feet from *a* trap!
114:9 I will please *the* Lord
in *the* land of *the* living.

Psalm 115:1 (KJV Ps 116)
Alleluia.
I believed
because of what I said,
yet I was greatly humiliated.
115:2 I said in my grief,
"Every man *is a* liar."

115:3 What
will I repay to *the* Lord
for all that He has paid to me?
115:4 I
will take security's cup,
and will invoke
the Lord's name.
115:5 I will pay my promises
to *the* Lord,
before all His people.

115:6 His holy ones' death
is precious
in *the* Lord's sight.
115:7 O Lord,
because I am Your slave –
I am Your slave and
Your slave woman's son –
You have broken
my chains.
115:8 I will sacrifice
offerings of praise to You.
I will invoke
in *the* Lord's name.
115:9 I will
pay my promises to *the* Lord,
before all His people,
115:10 in *the* courts

of *the* Lord's house,
in Your midst, Jerusalem.

Psalm 116:1 (KJV Ps 117)
Alleluia.
Praise *the* Lord, all nations!
Praise Him, all peoples,
116:2 because His mercy
is established over us!
His truth will endure
in *the* age.

Psalm 117:1 (KJV Ps 118)
Alleluia.
Confess to *the* Lord,
because *He is* good,
because His mercy
endures in *the* age!

117:2 Let Israel now speak,
because *He is* good,
because His mercy
endures in *the* age.
117:3 Let
Aaron's house now speak,
because His mercy
endures in *the* age.
117:4 Let those
who fear *the* Lord now speak,
because His mercy
endures in *the* age.

117:5 I invoked *the* Lord
from trouble,
and *the* Lord heard me
in broadness.
117:6 *The* Lord
is *a* helper to me.
I will not fear.
What can man do to me?
117:7 *The* Lord
is *a* helper to me,
and I will despise
my enemies.

117:8 *It is* better
to trust in *the* Lord
than to trust in man.

117:9 *It is* better
to hope in *the* Lord
than to hope in rulers.

117:10 All nations
surrounded me,
and in *the* Lord's name,
I was avenged against them.
117:11 Enveloping,
they besieged me.
But in *the* Lord's name,
I was avenged against them.
117:12 They
surrounded me like bees.
They blazed up
like fire among thorns.
And in *the* Lord's name,
I was avenged against them.
117:13 Shocked,
I was overthrown
that I might fall,
yet *the* Lord received me.

117:14 *The* Lord
is my strength and my praise,
and has become security
for me.
117:15 Rejoicing's voice
and security *are*
in *the* fair ones' tents.

117:16 *The* Lord's right hand
worked strength.
The Lord's right hand
lifted me up.
The Lord's right hand

worked strength.

117:17 I will not die,
but will live,
and I will tell *the* Lord's
works.
117:18 Punishing,
the Lord rebuked me.
Yet He did not hand me
over to death.

117:19 Open
to me fairness's gates.
Coming in through them,
I will confess to *the* Lord.
117:20 This
is the Lord's gate.
The fair will enter through it.

117:21 I will confess to You,
because You heard me.
You have become
security for me.
117:22 *A* stone
which builders rejected –
this has been made
into *a* cornerstone.
117:23 That was
done by *the* Lord.
This is wonderful in our eyes.
117:24 This is *the* day
which *the* Lord made.
May we exult
and be joyful in it.

117:25 Make secure, O Lord!
Make prosperous, O Lord!
117:26 One who is coming
in *the* Lord's name *is* blessed.
We have blessed you
from *the* Lord's house.
117:27 God is *the* Lord,
and He has enlightened us.
Set aside *the* day
for ceremony, in closeness,
even to *the* altar's horns!

117:28 You are my God,
and I will confess to You.
You are my God,
and I will lift You up.
I will confess to You,
because You heard me.
You have become
security for me.
117:29 Confess to *the* Lord,
because *He is* good,
because His mercy
endures in *the* age!

Psalm 118:1 (KJV Ps 119)
Alleluia.
Aleph.[76]

The unstained in *the* way
are blessed,
who walk in *the* Lord's law.
118:2 Those who study
His testimonies carefully
are blessed.
They seek Him
with all *the* heart.
118:3 For those
not working treachery
walk in His ways.
118:4 You have
commanded Your precepts
to be obeyed exceedingly.
118:5 If only they might
direct my ways
to keeping Your reasons,
118:6 then
I will not be dismayed –
when I have studied in all
Your precepts!
118:7 I will confess to You
in *the* heart's direction,
in that which I have learned
of Your fairness's judgment.
118:8 I
will keep Your reasons.

Do not abandon me
completely.

118:9 Beth.

In what can youth
correct its way?
In keeping Your words!
118:10 I sought You
with all my heart.
Do not turn me back
from Your precepts!
118:11 I hid
Your words in my heart,
that I not sin against You.
118:12 You
are blessed, Lord.
Teach me Your reasons!
118:13 I have
spoken with my lips
all Your mouth's judgments.
118:14 I delighted in Your
testimonies' way,
as in all riches.
118:15 I will
train in Your precepts.
I will consider Your ways.
118:16 I will meditate
on Your reasons.
I will not forget Your words.

118:17
Gimel

Pay Your slave back!

---

[76] This psalm in an acrostic poem. Each new section of the psalm begins with a succeeding letter in the Hebrew alphabet.

Revive me and I will keep
Your words!
118:18 Reveal to my eyes
and I will consider
Your law's wonders!
118:19 I am
a stranger in *the* land.
Do not hide Your precepts
from me!
118:20 My soul
longed to desire
Your reasons in all seasons.
118:21 You
rebuked *the* proud.
Those who turn away
from Your precepts
are cursed.
118:22 Take shame
and contempt away from me,
because I sought
Your testimonies!
118:23 For even princes sat
and spoke against me.
But Your slave practiced
in Your reasons.
118:24 For even
Your testimonies
are my meditation.
Your reasons *are* my counsel.

118:25
Daleth.

My soul stuck to *the* ground.
Revive me according to
Your word!

118:26 I
made my ways known,
and You heard me.
Teach me Your reasons!
118:27 Instruct me
in Your reasons' way,
and I will practice
in Your wonders!
118:28 My soul
slept before sadness.
Strengthen me in Your words!
118:29 Remove
a treacherous way from me!
Have mercy on me by
Your law!
118:30 I
have chosen truth's way.
I have not forgotten
Your judgments.
118:31 I clung
to Your testimonies, Lord.
Do not let me be dismayed!
118:32 I ran
in Your precepts' way,
when You widened my heart.

118:33
He.

Appoint to me *as* law
Your reason's way,
and I will seek it always!
118:34 Give
me understanding
and I will study Your law!
I will keep it in all my heart.

118:35 Lead me
in Your precepts' path,
because I have desired them!
118:36 Incline my heart
to Your testimonies,
and not to greed!
118:37 Turn my eyes away,
so I cannot see vanity!
Revive me in Your way!
118:38 Set Your word
before Your slave,
in fear of You!
118:39 Cut off my shame
because I am mistrusted,
for Your judgments
are pleasing!
118:40 Look!
I desired Your precepts.
Revive me in Your equity!

118:41
Vav.

May Your mercy
come over me, Lord –
Your security,
according to Your word,
118:42 and I
will respond in word
to those criticizing me,
because I have hoped
in Your words.
118:43 Do not
take truth's word
entirely away from my mouth,
because I have hoped
above all in Your judgments!
118:44 I will
always keep Your law,
in *the* age
and in *the* age of ages.
118:45 I will walk in
broadness because I sought
Your precepts.
118:46 I spoke
of Your testimonies
before kings,
and was not dismayed.
118:47 I meditated
in Your precepts,
in which I delighted.
118:48 I lifted up my hands
to *the* precepts which I loved.
I practiced in Your reasons.

118:49 Zai.

Be mindful of Your word
to Your slave,
in which You gave me hope!
118:50 This consoled me
in my humiliation,
because Your word
revived me.
118:51 *The* proud worked
treacherously completely,
but I have not turned away
from Your law.
118:52 I was mindful
of Your judgments
from *the* age, Lord,
and was consoled.

118:53 Weakness had me, before sinners abandoning Your law.
118:54 Your reasons were worthy of being sung by me in my pilgrimage's place.
118:55 I was mindful of Your name in *the* night, Lord, and I kept Your law.
118:56 This was done for me, because I sought Your reasons

118:57
Heth.

The Lord *is* my portion. I said, 'Let Your law be kept!'
118:58 I prayed before Your face with all my heart. Have mercy on me, according to Your word!
118:59 I considered my ways, and You turned my feet to Your testimonies.
118:60 I was ready and was not troubled, so I could keep Your precepts.
118:61 Sinners ropes bound me, yet I did not forget Your law.
118:62 In *the* middle of *the* night I rose up to confess to You, because of Your reasons' judgments.
118:63 I am *a* partaker with all who fear You, and who keep Your precepts.
118:64 *The* land is full of *the* Lord's mercy. Teach me Your reasons!

118:65
Teth.

You made goodness for Your slave, Lord, according to Your word.
118:66 Teach me goodness, discipline, and knowledge, because I believed Your precepts!
118:68 Before I was humbled I fell short. For this reason I guarded Your word.
118:69 You are good. In Your goodness teach me Your reasons!
118:69 Proud men's treachery was multiplied over me, but I, with all my heart, will study Your precepts.
118:70 Their heart was congealed like milk. I, truly, have meditated on Your law.
118:71 *It was* good to me

that You humbled me,
so I can learn Your reasons.
118:72 Your mouth's law
is good to me,
better than thousands
in gold and silver.

118:73
Ioth.

Your hands made me
and formed me.
Give me understanding
and I will learn Your
precepts!
118:74 Those who fear You
will see me and rejoice,
because I hoped above all
in Your words.
118:75 I understood, Lord,
because Your judgments
are fair.
You humbled me by truth.
118:76 Let
Your mercy appear,
so it can console me
according to Your word
to Your slave.
118:77 Let
Your compassions
come to me and I will live,
because Your law
is my meditation.
118:78 Let
the proud be dismayed,
because they unfairly
worked betrayal against me.
But I will train in Your
precepts.
118:79 Turn
those fearing You back to me,
and those who have known
Your testimonies!
118:80 May my heart
be spotless in Your reasons,
that I not be dismayed.

118:81
Caf.

My soul has grown weak
in Your security.
I hoped above all
in Your word.
118:82 My eyes grew weak
in Your word, saying,
'When will You comfort me,'
118:83 because I became
like skin in frost.
I have not forgotten
Your reasons.
118:84 How many days
are *there* for Your slave?
When will You
make judgment against those
persecuting me?
118:85 Betrayers
have told me fables,
but Your law *is* not like *that*.
118:86 All
Your precepts *are* truth.
Others have persecuted

me treacherously.
Help me!
118:87 They almost
consumed me in *the* land,
yet I have not abandoned
Your precepts.
118:88 Revive me,
according to Your mercy,
and I will keep
Your mouth's testimony!

118:89
Lamed.

Your word endures
in eternity, Lord, in *the* sky.
118:90 Your truth *remains*
in generation after generation.
You established *the* land
and it endures.
118:91 Day continues
by Your command,
for all *things* serve You.
118:92 If not that Your law
is my meditation,
then perhaps
I would have perished
in my humiliation.
118:93 I will not forget
Your reasons in eternity,
because by these
You revived me.
118:94 I am Yours.
Make me secure,
for I sought Your reasons!
118:95 Sinners waited for me,
so they could destroy me.
I understood Your
testimonies.
118:96 I have seen *an* end
to every consummation.
Your commandment
is exceedingly wide.

118:97
Mem.

How I delighted in Your law!
It is my meditation all day.
118:98 You made me more
prudent than my enemies,
by Your commandment,
because *they are* with me
in eternity.
118:99 I understood more
than all those teaching me,
because my meditation
is Your testimonies.
118:100 I
understood more than *the* old,
because I sought
Your precepts.
118:101 I kept my feet
from every harmful path,
so I can keep Your words.
118:102 I
have not turned away
from Your judgments,
because You placed Your law
in me.
118:103 How sweet *is*

Your word to my throat!
It is sweeter than honey
to my mouth.
118:104 I understood
from Your precepts.
Because of this I hated
every treacherous way.

118:105
Nun.

Your word is lamp
to my feet
and light to my path.
118:106 I
have sworn and stood
to keep Your fairness's
judgments.
118:107 I was humiliated
completely, Lord.
Revive me, according to
Your word!
118:108 Make
my lips' free offerings
well-pleasing, Lord,
and teach me Your
judgments!
118:109 My soul
is always in my hands,
yet I have not forgotten
Your law.
118:110 Sinners
placed a trap for me,
yet I did not wander
from Your precepts.
118:111 I
acquired Your testimonies
by inheritance in eternity,
because they are
my heart's exultation.
118:112 I inclined my heart
to working Your reasons
in eternity,
because of *the* reward.

118:113
Samech.

I held betrayers in hatred,
yet I delighted in Your law.
118:114 Your are
my helper and my sustainer.
I hoped above all
in Your word.
118:115 Turn away
from me, malignant *ones*,
and I will study
my God's precepts!
118:116 Accept me
according to Your word
and I will live!
Do not dismay me
in my expectation!
118:117 Help me
and I will be secure,
and I will meditate
in Your reasons always!
118:118 You scorned
all who turn away
from Your justices,
because their thought
is unfair.

118:119 I considered
all *the* land's sinners as liars.
Therefore, I delighted
in Your testimonies.
118:120 Pierce my flesh
with Your fear,
for I feared Your judgments!

118:121
Ain.

I worked judgment
and fairness.
Do not hand me over
to those accusing me falsely!
118:122 Sustain
Your slave in good!
Do not let *the* proud
oppress me!
118:123 May eyes faltered
in Your security,
and in Your fairness's word.
118:124 Do with Your slave
according to Your mercy!
Teach me Your reasons!
118:125 I am Your slave.
Give me understanding,
and I will know Your
testimonies!
118:126 *It is* time
for working by *the* Lord
They have wasted Your law.
118:127 Therefore,
I delighted in Your precepts,
more than gold and topaz.
118:128 Because of this,
I was directed toward
all Your precepts.
I hated every treacherous way.

118:129
Fe.

Your testimonies
are miraculous.
Therefore my soul
studied them.
118:130 Your word's
declaration enlightens and
gives understanding
to little *ones*.
118:131 I opened my mouth
and drew in breath,
because I desired
Your precepts.
118:132 Look on me
and have mercy on me,
according to *the* judgment
of those who fear Your name!
118:133 Guide my steps
according to Your word,
and may every injustice
not rule over me!
118:134 Buy me back
from man's false accusations,
and I will keep Your precepts!
118:135 Light up Your face
over Your slave,
and teach me Your reasons!
118:136 My eyes led me out
of *the* water's mouth,

because *others* did not keep
Your law.

118:137
Sade.

Lord, You are fair
and Your judgment *is* right.
118:138 You
commanded fairness
as Your testimonies
and *as* Your truth, greatly.
118:139 My zeal
made me dry up,
because my enemies
have forgotten Your words.
118:140 Your word
burned fiercely,
and Your slave delighted
in it.
118:141 I
am young and despised.
I have not forgotten
Your reasons.
118:142 Your fairness
is fairness in eternity,
and Your law *is* truth.
118:143 Trouble
and anxiety found me.
Your precepts *are*
my meditation.
118:144 Your testimonies
are equity in eternity.
Give me understanding
and I will live!

118:145
Cof.

I cried out with all *my* heart.
Hear me, Lord!
I will seek all Your reasons.
118:146 I cried out to You.
Make me secure,
and I will keep Your precepts!
118:147 I arrived
at maturity and cried out.
I hoped above all
in Your words.
118:148 My eyes
awakened at daybreak,
so I could consider
Your words.
118:149 Hear my voice
according to Your mercy,
Lord!
According to Your judgment,
revive me!
118:150 Those
persecuting me came near
me treacherously,
but they have become
far from Your law.
118:151 You are near, Lord,
and all Your ways *are* truth.
118:152 I
learned Your testimonies
from *the* beginning,
because You established them
in eternity.

118:153
Res.

See my humiliation
and rescue me,
because I have not forgotten
Your law!
118:154 Judge my judgment,
and buy me back!
According to Your word,
revive me!
118:155 Security
is far from sinners,
because they have not
sought Your reasons.
118:156 Your
mercies are many, Lord.
Revive me according to
Your judgments!
118:157 *There are* many
who persecute me
and trouble me.
I have not turned away
from Your testimonies.
118:158 I saw liars
and wasted away,
because they did not guard
Your words.
118:159 See, Lord,
because I delighted
in Your precepts!
Revive me in Your mercy!
118:160 Your
words' beginning *is* truth.
All Your judgments
show Your fairness
in eternity.

118:161
Sen.

Princes persecuted me
without cause,
yet my heart feared
for Your words.
118:162 I will be happy
over Your words
like one who finds
many spoils.
118:163 I hated treachery
and was scorned,
but I delighted in Your law.
118:164 Seven times
each day, I have spoken
praise to You, because of
Your fairness's judgment.
118:165 Great peace *comes*
to those who are devoted
to Your law.
There is no scandal for them.
118:166 I waited
for Your security, Lord,
and I delighted
in Your precepts.
118:167 My soul
kept Your testimonies
and delighted fiercely
in them.
118:168 I
served Your precepts
and Your testimonies,
because all my ways

are in Your sight.

118:169
Thau.

May my plea come near,
into Your sight, Lord!
Give me understanding,
along with Your word!
118:170 May my request
enter in Your sight.
According to Your word,
rescue me!
118:171 My lips
will sing *a* hymn,
when You teach me
Your reasons.
118:172 My tongue
will pronounce Your word,
because all Your precepts
are fairness.
118:173 Let Your hand work,
so it can make me secure,
because I have chosen
Your precepts.
118:174 I longed
for Your security, Lord,
and Your law *is*
my meditation.
118:175 My soul will live
and will praise You,
and Your judgments
will help me.
118:176 I wandered like
a sheep which has perished.
Seek Your slave,
because I have not forgotten
Your precepts!

Psalm 119:1 (KJV Ps 120)
A processional song

I called out to *the* Lord
when I was troubled,
and He heard me.
119:2 Lord, free my soul
from betraying lips,
from *a* lying tongue!
119:3 What can he offer You,
and what can he set
before You?
To *a* lying tongue
119:4 *He will offer*
the powerful's sharp arrows,
with desolation's burning
coals!
119:5 Woe to me,
because my stay is prolonged!
I lived with Cedar's[77]
inhabitants.
119:6 My soul
was long housed
119:7 with those
who hate peace.
I was peaceful
when I spoke to them.
They fought against me
without cause.

Psalm 120:1 (KJV Ps 121)
A processional song.

I lifted up my eyes
to *the* mountains?
Where will help
come to me from?
120:2 My help
comes from *the* Lord,
who made sky and land.
120:3 May He not surrender
Your foot into commotion,
nor may He who guards you
sleep.
120:4 Look,
He who guards Israel
will not doze off or sleep,
120:5 *The* Lord guards you.
The Lord *is* your protection,
over your right *hand*.
120:6 Sun
will not burn you by day,
nor moon by night.
120:7 *The* Lord
guards you from all harm.
May *the* Lord guard your soul!
120:8 May *the* Lord
guard your entering
and your leaving,
from this *moment* now
and even in *the* age!

---

[77] Cedar as an individual is first mentioned in scripture at Genesis 25:13. Cedar's inhabitants were known for being warlike.

Psalm 121:1 (KJV Ps 122)
A processional song,
of David himself.

I was happy with those
who said to me,
"Let us go to *the* Lord's
house."
121:2 Our feet were standing
in your courts, Jerusalem –
121:3 Jerusalem,
which is built
like *a* city whose sharing
is in *the* thing itself.
121:4 For there tribes go up –
the Lord's tribes,
Israel's testimony –
to *the* confessing
of *the* Lord's name.
121:5 For there thrones
were set in judgment,
thrones over David's house.
121:6 Ask for
those *things* which *lead*
to Jerusalem's peace,
to *the* abundance of those
delighting in you!

121:7 May peace be
in your strength,
and abundance in
your towers!
121:8 For my brothers' sake
and my neighbors,
I spoke peace from you.
121:9 For *the* sake
of *the* Lord our God's house,
I sought good for you.

Psalm 122:1 (KJV Ps 123)
A processional song.

I lifted up my eyes to You,
who live in *the* sky.
122:2 Look, like slaves' eyes
on their masters' hands,
like slave women's eyes
on their mistresses' hands,
so our eyes *are* on
the Lord our God,
until He has mercy on us!

122:3 Have
mercy with us, Lord,
have mercy,
because we are full
of much contempt,
122:4 because our soul is full
of much reproach
from *the* prosperous,
and *from the* prideful's
disdain!

Psalm 123:1 (KJV Ps 124)
A processional song,
of David himself.

"Had *the* Lord
not been among us,"
let Israel now say,
123:2 "Had *the* Lord
not been among us,
when men rose up against us,
123:3 "perhaps they would
have swallowed us alive –
when their fury was enraged
against us.
123:4 "Perhaps water
would have overwhelmed us.
123:5 "Our soul
passed through *a* torrent.
Perhaps our soul
would have passed through
an intolerable flood.

123:6 "Blessed be *the* Lord,
who has not given us
into their teeth's deceit.
123:7 "Our soul,
like *a* sparrow,
was snatched away
from *the* hunter's snare.
The snare was destroyed
and we were freed.
123:8 "Our help *is*
in the Lord's name,
who made sky and land."

Psalm 124:1 (KJV Ps 125)
A processional psalm.

Those who trust in *the* Lord
are like Mount Sion.
He will not be moved
in eternity, who lives
124:2 in Jerusalem.
Mountains *are* around it,
and *the* Lord *is* around
its people,
from this *moment* now
and even in *the* age.
124:3 For He will not
leave behind *the* sinners' rod
over *the* fair ones'
inheritance,
so *the* fair will not
stretch out their hands
to treachery.

124:4 Do good, Lord,
to *the* good,
and to *the* straightforward
in heart!
124:5 But to
those turning away
in *their* obligations –
the Lord will lead *them* away
with those who
work treachery.

Peace *be* over Israel!

Psalm 125:1 (KJV Ps 126)
A processional song.

In *the* Lord's turning back
Sion's captivity,
we became like
those who are consoled.
125:2 Then our mouth
was filled with joy,
and our tongue
with exultation.
Then let them say
among nations,
"The Lord has magnified
His work with them."

125:3 *The* Lord has
magnified *His* work with us.
We have become
those rejoicing.
125:4 Turn back
our captivity, Lord,
like *a* flood in *the* south.[78]

125:5 Those who sow in tears
will reap in exultation.
125:6 Going out,
they went and wept,
carrying their seed.
But coming in,
they will come
in exultation,
carrying their bundles.

---

[78] The south, for Israel, was the Negev, a harsh, desert region.

Psalm 126:1 (KJV Ps 127)
A processional song,
of Solomon.

Unless *the* Lord
builds *the* house,
those who build it
have labored in vain.
Unless *the* Lord guards *a* city,
one who guards *it*
has watched pointlessly.
126:2 *It* is pointless for you
to get up before light,
to rise up after
you have sat down –
you who eat sorrow's bread –
when He will give sleep
to His loved *ones*.

126:3 Look, *the* Lord's
inheritance *is* children,
the womb's fruit *His* goods.
126:4 Like arrows
in *the* mighty's hands,
so *the* children
of those shaken.
126:5 Blessed is *a* man
who will fill his desire
from them.
He will not be dismayed
when his enemies speak
in *the* gate.

Psalm 127:1 (KJV Ps 128)
A processional psalm.

Blessed are all
who fear *the* Lord,
who walk in His ways.
127:2 Because
you have eaten
your hands' hard work,
you are blessed,
and *it* will be well with you.
127:3 Your wife *will be*
like *a* fruitful vine
on your house's sides.
Your children *will be*
like *an* olive nursery
around your table.
127:4 Look,
in this way is *a* man
who fears *the* Lord blessed!

127:5 May *the* Lord
bless you from Sion!
May you see
Jerusalem's good blessings
all your life's days!
127:6 May you see
your children's children!
Peace *be* over Israel!

Psalm 128:1 (KJV Ps 129) *A* processional psalm.

"They fought against me
often since my youth,"
let Israel now say.
128:2 "They
fought against me
often since my youth,
though they were unable
to *conquer* me.
128:3 "Sinners built up
against my back.
They prolonged
their treachery.
128:4 *"The* just Lord
will break sinners' necks.
128:5 "May all
who hated Sion
be dismayed and turned back!
128:6 "May they be
like grass on rooftops,
which dries up
before it can grow,
128:7 "from
which one who reaps
and one who gathers bundles
does not fill his hand –
128:8 "and
those who passed by
did not say,
'*The* Lord's blessing
is over you.
We have blessed you
in *the* Lord's name.'"

Psalm 129:1 (KJV Ps 130)
A processional psalm

I cried out to You
from *the* depths, Lord.
129:2 Lord, hear my voice!
Let Your ears be attentive
to my petitions' voice!
129:3 If you watch
treacheries, Lord,
Lord, who will sustain –
129:4 because
atonement is with You?
I sustained you, Lord,
according to Your law.
My soul sustained
in Your word.

129:5 My soul
hoped in *the* Lord.
129:6 Let Israel
hope in *the* Lord
from morning watch
even to night,
129:7 because mercy
is with the Lord,
and abundant redemption
at His side.
129:8 He will buy Israel back
from all its treacheries.

Psalm 130:1 (KJV Ps 131)
A processional song,
of David.

Lord, my heart
was not lifted up,
nor were my eyes led out,
nor did I walk in greatness,
nor in wonders above me.
130:2 If I did not feel humbly
but lifted up my soul,
like *a* nursing baby
on its mother,
so *may the* reward *be*
in my soul.
130:3 Let Israel
hope in *the* Lord,
from this *moment* now
and even in *the* age.

Psalm 131:1 (KJV Ps 132)
A processional song.

Remember David, Lord,
and all his gentleness,
131:2 as he
swore to *the* Lord!
"I promised *a* vow
to Jacob's God,
131:3 "if I will enter
into my house's dwelling,
if I will climb
into my bed's cover –
131:4 "if I
will give my eyes sleep,
or my eyelids slumber –
131:5 "or rest to my times,
until I have found
the Lord *a* place –
a dwelling for Jacob's God."

131:6 Look,
we heard it in Ephratha!
We found it in *the* forest's
fields.
131:7 We
entered into his dwelling.
We worshiped in *the* place
where he placed His feet.

131:8 Rise, Lord,
in Your rest,
You and *the* Ark

of Your sanctifications![79]
131:9 May Your priests
be clothed with fairness,
and Your holy *ones* exult.

131:10 For David,
Your slave's, sake,
do not turn Your Christ's face
away!
131:11 *The* Lord
has sworn truth to David
and will not frustrate him:
"I will place *one*
from your womb's fruit
over your throne.
131:12 "If your children
will keep my testament
and my testimonies –
these which I will teach them
and their children –
they will sit on your throne
even in *the* age."

131:13 For *the* Lord
chose Sion.
He chose it as *a* dwelling
for Himself.
131:14 "This is my rest
in *the* age of ages.
I will live here, for I chose it.
131:15 "Blessing
its widows, I will bless.
I will fill its poor with bread.

131:16 "I will
dress its priests with security.
Its holy ones will exult
with great joy.
131:17 "There I will
bring out David's strength.
I have prepared *a* lamp
for Christ's light.
131:18 "I will dress
his enemies in confusion,
but my sanctification
will flourish over him."

---

[79] The story of Israel's Ark of the Covenant begins in Exodus 25.

Psalm 132:1 (KJV Ps 133)
A processional song,
of David.

Look – how good
and how pleasant
for brothers to live as one!
132:2 *It is*
like oil on *the* head,
which drips down
on *the* beard –
Aaron's beard –
which drips down
on his clothes' fringe –
132:3 like Hermon's dew,
which drips down
into Sion's mountains,
because there *the* Lord
has commanded
blessing and life,
even in *the* age!

Psalm 133:1 (KJV Ps 134)
A processional song.

Look, bless *the* Lord now,
all *the* Lord's slaves –
you who are standing
in *the* Lord's house,
in *the* courts of our God's
house!
133:2 Lift up your hands
by night in *the* holy place,
and bless *the* Lord!
133:3 May *the* Lord
who made sky and land
bless you from Sion.

Psalm 134:1 (KJV Ps 135)
Alleluia.

Praise *the* Lord's name!
Praise *the* Lord,
you slaves –
134:2 you who stand
in *the* Lord's house,
in *the* courts
of our God's house!
134:3 Praise *the* Lord,
because *the* Lord *is* good!
Chant psalms to His name,
because *it is* pleasant –
134:4 because *the* Lord
chose Jacob for Himself,
Israel as *a* possession
for Himself!
134:5 For I have known
that *the* Lord is great.
Our God *stands* before
all gods.

134:6 All that He willed
the Lord did –
in sky and in land,
in sea and in all abysses.
134:7 Leading out clouds
from land's end,
He made lightnings in rain.
He produces winds
from His treasuries –
134:8 who
struck Egypt's firstborn,
from men even to cattle.

134:9 He sent out
signs and wonders
in your midst, Egypt –
against Pharaoh and against
all his slaves –
134:10 who struck down
many nations
and killed mighty kings –
134:11 Sion,
the Amorites' king,
Og, Bashan's king,
and all of Canaan's kings.
134:12 He gave their land
as an inheritance,
Israel's inheritance –
His people.

134:13 Lord, Your name
endures in eternity.
Lord, Your memory
lives in generation
after generation,
134:14 because *the* Lord
will judge His people,
and will be prayed to
among His slaves.

134:15 *The* nations' images
are silver and god,
works of human hands.
134:16 They have *a* mouth,
yet will not speak.
They have eyes,
yet will not see.
134:17 They have ears,
yet will not hear,

for neither is breath
in their mouth.
134:18 May those
who make them
become like them –
and all who hope in them.

134:19 Israel's
house, bless *the* Lord!
Aaron's house, bless *the* Lord!
134:20 Levi's
house, bless *the* Lord!
You who fear *the* Lord,
bless *the* Lord!
134:21 *The* Lord,
who lives in Jerusalem,
be blessed from Sion!

Psalm 135:1 (KJV Ps 136)
Alleluia.

Confess to *the* Lord,
because He is good,
because His mercy
lives in eternity!
135:2 Confess
to *the* gods' God,
because His mercy
lives in eternity!
135:3 Confess
to *the* lords' Lord,
because His mercy
lives in eternity;
135:4 who alone works
great wonders,
because His mercy
lives in eternity;
135:5 who made skies
in understanding,
because His mercy
lives in eternity;
135:6 who established
land over waters,
because His mercy
lives in eternity;
135:7 who made great lights,
because His mercy
lives in eternity;
135:8 Sun in day's power,
because His mercy
lives in eternity;
135:9 moon and stars
in night's power,
because His mercy

lives in eternity;
135:10 who struck Egypt
with their firstborn,
because His mercy
lives in eternity;
135:11 who led Israel out
from among them,
because His mercy
lives in eternity;
135:12 with *a* mighty hand
and *an* arm lifted high,
because His mercy
lives in eternity;
135:13 who divided
the Red Sea in divisions,
because His mercy
lives in eternity;
135:14 and led Israel
through its midst,
because His mercy
lives in eternity;
135:15 and shook
off Pharaoh and his army
into *the* Red Sea,
because His mercy
lives in eternity;
135:16 who led His people
across *the* desert,
because His mercy
lives in eternity;
135:17 who
struck down great kings,
because His mercy
lives in eternity;
135:18 and killed
mighty kings,
because His mercy
lives in eternity;
135:19 Sion,
the Amorites' king,
because His mercy
lives in eternity;
135:20 and Og,
Bashan's king,
because His mercy
lives in eternity;
135:21 and gave their land
as an inheritance,
because His mercy
lives in eternity;
135:22 *an* inheritance
to Israel, His slave,
because His mercy
lives in eternity;
135:23 because
in our humiliation,
He was mindful of us,
because His mercy
lives in eternity;
135:24 and bought us back
from our enemies,
because His mercy
lives in eternity;
135:25 who gives
food to all flesh,
because His mercy
lives in eternity!

135:26 Confess
to *the* sky's God,
because His mercy
lives in eternity!

Confess to *the* lords' Lord,
because His mercy
lives in eternity!

Psalm 136:1 (KJV Ps 137)
David, of Jeremiah.

Over Babylon's rivers,
there we sat and wept
when we remembered Sion.
136:2 In willows, in its midst,
we hung up our instruments,
136:3 because there
they asked us –
those who led us captive –
the words of songs.
Those who kidnaped us said,
"Sing us *a* hymn
from Sion's songs."

136:4 How will we
sing *the* Lord's song
in *a* strange land?
136:5 If I
forget you, Jerusalem,
may my right *hand*
be given over to oblivion!
136:6 May my tongue
stick to my jaws
if I do not remember you –
if I do not place Jerusalem
at my happiness's beginning!

136:7 Be mindful, Lord,
of Edom's children,
who say *on* Jerusalem's day,
"Rob it, rob it –
even to its foundations!"
136:8 Babylon's
miserable daughter,

one who pays back to you
what you have paid others
will be blessed!
136:9 *One* who will take
and crush your little ones
against *a* rock
will be blessed!

Psalm 137:1 (KJV Ps 138)
Of David himself.

I will confess to You, Lord,
in all my heart,
because You heard
my mouth's words.
I will chant psalms to You
in *the* angels' sight.
137:2 I will worship
toward Your holy temple
and confess Your name
because of Your mercy
and Your truth,
because You have lifted up
over all things Your holy
name.
137:3 In whatever day
I invoke You, hear me!
You will multiply me
in my soul's strength.

137:4 May all *the* land's
kings confess to *the* Lord,
because they have heard
all Your mouth's words.
137:5 May they sing
in *the* Lord's ways,
because *the* Lord's glory
is great.
137:6 For *the* Lord *is*
lifted up and looks
on *the* humble,
yet He knows *the* important
from far away.

137:7 If I
walk in trouble' midst,
You will revive me.
You stretched out Your hand
against my enemies' anger,
and Your right hand
made me secure.
137:8 *The* Lord
will repay on my behalf.
Lord, Your mercy *endures*
in *the* age.
Do not despise
Your hands' work!

Psalm 138:1 (KJV Ps 139)
To *the* end.
A psalm of David.

138:2 Lord, You proved me
and have known me.
You knew my sitting down
and my rising up.
138:3 You understood
my thoughts from far away.
You searched my path
and my line.
138:4 You saw beforehand
all my ways,
because *there* is no word
on my tongue.[80]
138:5 Look, Lord,
You have known all –
the latest and *the* ancient.
You formed me
and placed Your hand
over me.
138:6 Your knowledge
has become wondrous.
It is strengthened greatly,
apart from me.
I will not be able
to *approach* it.

138:7 Where will I go
apart from Your Spirit?
Where will I flee

---

[80] Compare to RSV, " Even before a word is on my tongue, lo, O LORD, thou knowest it altogether."

from Your face?
138:8 If I
will climb up to *the* sky,
You are there.
If I will climb down
to *the* inferno,
You are present.
138:9 If I
take up my wings at daybreak
and live in *the* sea's ends,
138:10 even there,
Your hand will lead me,
and Your right hand
will hold me.

138:11 I said,
"Perhaps shadows
will trample me,
and night *obscure* light
in my delights."
138:12 *Yet* shadows will not
conceal *things* from You,
and night, like day,
will be lit up.
As His darkness *is,*
so also His light.

138:13 For You
have taken hold of my insides.
You received me
from my mother's uterus.[81]
138:14 I will confess You,
because You are lifted up
overwhelmingly.
Your works are wonderful,
and my soul
recognizes *it* exceedingly.

138:15 My bone
is not hidden from You,
which You formed in secret,
and my substance
in *the* land's lower parts.
138:16 Your eyes saw
my incompleteness,
and all will be written
in Your book.
Days will be formed,
and no one in them.[82]

138:17 Yet with me,
Your friends are honored
exceedingly, *O* God.
Their rule is established
exceedingly.
138:18 I will number them,
and they will be multiplied
above sand.
I have risen up
and am still with You.

138:19 If *only* You
would kill sinners, God!

---

[81] Compare to RSV: "For thou didst form my inward parts, thou didst knit me together in my mother's womb."

[82] Compare to RSV: "Thy eyes beheld my unformed substance; in thy book were written, every one of them, the days that were formed for me, when as yet there was none of them."

Turn away from me,
bloody men.!
138:20 For you
say in thought,
'They will capture Your cities
in vain.'
138:21 Do I not hate those
who hate You, Lord?
And have I *not* wasted away
over your enemies?
138:22 I hate them
with total hatred.
They became my enemies.

138:23 Prove me, God,
and know my heart!
Question me
and know my paths!
138:24 See if *there is*
a treacherous way in me,
and led me in *the* eternal way!

Psalm 139:1 (KJV Ps 140)
To *the* end,
a psalm of David.

139:2 Rescue me, Lord,
from *a* harmful man!
Deliver me
from *a* treacherous man!
139:3 Those who considered
betrayals in *their* heart –
all day they arranged battles.
139:4 Their tongue
was forked like snakes.
Asps' venom *was*
beneath their lips.
139:5 Keep me, Lord,
from sinners' hands!
Rescue me
from treacherous men,
who plot to undermine
my steps!
139:6 *The* proud
hid *a* trap for me.
They stretched out ropes
in *a* trap beside *the* way.
They put *a* stumbling block
in front of me.

139:7 I said to *the* Lord,
"You are my God.
Hear, Lord, my petition's
voice!
139:8 "Lord, Lord,
strength of my security,
You covered my head
on *the* day of war.

139:9 "Do not hand over
my desire to sinners, Lord!
They plotted against me.
Do not abandon me,
unless perhaps
they be lifted up!"

139:10 Their head
is around them.
Their lips' labor
will cover them.
139:11 Burning coals
will fall on them.
You will throw them down
in fire.
They will not stand
in miseries.
139:12 *A* blabbering man
will not be guided
in *the* land.
Harm will capture
an unfair one in destruction.
139:13 I understood
that *the* Lord will work
judgment for *the* powerless,
and revenge for *the* poor.

139:14 Even so, *the* fair
will confess Your name.
The honest will live
with Your face.

Psalm 140:1 (KJV Ps 141)
A psalm of David.

Lord, I cried out to You.
Hear me!
Understand my voice
when I cry to You.
140:2 May my prayer
be directed like incense
in Your sight,
the raising of my hands
like *the* evening sacrifice.

140:3 Place, Lord,
a guard on my mouth,
and *a* doorway
around my lips!
140:4 Do not
turn my heart away
in harmful words,
toward excusing sins'
excuses,
with men working treachery!
I will not communicate
with their chosen *ones*!

140:5 *A* fair one
will correct me in mercy
and rebuke me,
but sinners' oil
will not soothe my head,
because even to this moment
my prayer *is* against
what pleases them.
140:6 Their judges were
overwhelmed beside *a* rock.

They will hear my words,
because they could.
140:7 As *the*
earth's thickness
is thrown up over *the* land,
our bones are scattered
beside *the* inferno.

140:8 Yet my eyes
are on You, Lord.
I hoped in You.
Do not carry my soul away!
140:9 Keep me from *the* trap
which they set against me,
and from *the* scandals
of those practicing betrayal!
140:10 Sinners will fall
in their *own* net,
I am set apart
until I may pass through.

Psalm 141:1 (KJV Ps 142)
David's understanding,
a prayer when he was
in *the* cave.[83]

141:2 I cried out
by my voice to *the* Lord.
By my voice, I pleaded
with *the* Lord.
141:3 I pour out
my petition in His sight.
I tell my trouble before Him,
141:4 in my spirit's falling
away from me.

You have know my paths.
They hid *a* trap against me
in *the* way here
which I walked.
141:5 I looked
to *the* right and I saw.
There was no one
who would acknowledge me.
Escape has perished for me,
and *there* is no one
who seeks my soul.

141:6 I
cried out to You, Lord.
I said, "You are my hope –
my portion in *the* living's
land."
141:7 Understand my plea,

---

[83] See 1 Samuel 24.

because I am greatly
humiliated!
Free me from those
persecuting me,
because they are strengthened
against me!
141:8 Lead my soul out
from custody,
to Your name's confessing!
The fair are waiting for me,
until You repay me.

Psalm 142:1 (KJV Ps 143)
A psalm of David,
when his son pursued him.

Lord, hear my prayer!
Listen with ears
to my petition!
In Your truth,
hear me in Your fairness!
142:2 Do not enter into
judgment with Your slave,
because no one living
will be justified in Your sight!
142:3 For *an* enemy
is pursuing my soul.
He humiliated my life
in *the* land.
He put me in shadows,
like those dead from *the* age.
142:4 My spirit
is anxious over me.
My heart is troubled
within me.

142:5 I am
mindful of ancient days.
I meditated on all
Your works.
I thought deeply about
all Your hands' actions.
142:6 I stretched out
my hands to You.
My soul *cried out* to You
like waterless land.

142:7 Hear me quickly, Lord!

My spirit has failed.
Do not turn Your face
away from me,
or I will be like those
going down into *the* pit!
142:8 Make Your mercy
audible to me early,
because I have hoped in You!
Make known to me
the way which I should walk,
because I lifted up
my soul to You!
142:9 Rescue me
from my enemies, Lord!
I fled to You.
142:10 Teach me
to do Your will,
because You are my God!
Your good Spirit
will lead me
into *an* honest land.

142:11 For Your
name's sake, Lord, revive me
in Your fairness!
May You lead my soul
out of trouble.
142:12 In Your mercy,
You will scatter my enemies
and destroy all those
who trouble my soul,
because I am Your slave.

Psalm 143:1 (KJV Ps 144)
Of David, against Goliath.

The Lord my God *is* blessed,
who trains my hands
for battle,
my fingers for war –
143:2 my mercy
and my refuge, my sustainer
and my liberator,
my protector!
I hoped in Him,
who places my people
under me.

143:3 Lord, what is man
that You became known
to him,
or man's son that You
consider him?
143:4 Man
has become like vanity.
His days pass away
like shadows.

143:5 Lord, bend down
Your skies and descend!
Touch mountains
and they will smoke!
143:6 Lightnings flashing,
You will scatter them.
Send out Your arrows
and You will trouble them!
143:7 Send out Your hand
from on high!
Rescue me and free me

from many waters,
from *the* hands
of foreigners' children –
143:8 whose
mouth spoke vanity,
and their right hand
is betrayal's right hand!

143:9 God, I will sing
a new song to You.
I will chant psalms to You
on a ten-stringed harp –
143:10 who gives
security to kings,
who redeems David,
His slave, from *a* malignant
sword.

143:11 Rescue me!
Snatch me away
from *the* hands
of foreigners' children,
whose mouth spoke vanity,
and their right *hand*
is betrayal's right *hand*!
143:12 *Their*[84] sons
are like tender seedlings
in their youth;
their daughters
adorned all around
in *a* temple's likeness.
143:13 Their
storerooms *are* full,
bringing out this into that;
their sheep bearing
many lambs,
abundant in their going out;
143:14 their cattle fat.
There is no ruined wall
or crossing,
nor outcry in their streets.

143:15 They called
a people blessed
who have these *things*.
A people *is* blessed, though,
to whom *the* Lord *is* God.

---

[84] Literally, "Whose sons . . ."

Psalm 144:1 (KJV Ps 145)
David's praise.

I will exalt You,
God my King,
and will bless Your name –
in *the* age,
and in *the* age of ages.
144:2 I will bless you
and praise Your name
through each day,
in *the* age,
and in *the* age of ages.

144:3 *The* Lord is great
and exceedingly praiseworthy.
There is no end
of His greatness.
144:4 Generation
after generation
will praise Your works,
and tell Your power.
144:5 They will speak
of Your glorious holiness's
magnificence,
and will tell Your wonders.
144:6 They will speak
Your terrible strength,
and tell Your greatness.
144:7 They will bring out
the memory of
Your abundant sweetness,
and will rejoice
in Your fairness.

144:8 *The* Lord is
compassionate and merciful,
patient and greatly merciful.
144:9 *The* Lord
is pleasing to all.
His compassions *abide*
over all His works.

144:10 May all Your works
confess to You, Lord,
and all Your holy ones
confess to You.
144:11 May they speak
of Your reign's glory,
and talk of Your power,
144:12 so they can make
Your power known
to men's children,
and *the* fame
of Your magnificent reign.

144:13 Your kingdom
is a kingdom in all ages.
Your rule *endures*
among every generation
and race.
The Lord *is* faithful
in all His words,
and holy in all His works.
144:14 *The* Lord
comforts all who fall,
and lifts up all
who *are* crushed.
144:15 *The* eyes
of all hope in You,
and You give their food

in *a* timely season.
144:16 You
open Your hand
and fill every soul
with blessing.

144:17 *The* Lord *is* fair
in all His ways,
and holy in all His works.
144:18 *The* Lord is near
to all who invoke Him,
all who invoke Him in truth.
144:19 He will do *the* will
of those fearing Him.
He will hear their plea,
and will make them secure.

144:20 *The* Lord guards
all those delighting in Him,
and will ruin all sinners.
144:21 My mouth will speak
the Lord's praise.
Let all flesh bless
His holy name in *the* age,
and in *the* age of ages.

Psalm 145:1 (KJV Ps 146)
Alleluia.
Of Haggai and Zachariah.

Praise, my soul, *the* Lord!
145:2 I will praise
the Lord in my life.
I will chant psalms
to my God as long
as I am.

145:3 Do not trust in princes,
in men's children,
in whom *there* is no security!
145:4 His breath will go out
and return to his dust.
In that day, all their plots
will perish.

145:5 Blessed *is* one
to whom Jacob's God
is his helper!
His help will be
in *the* Lord Himself,
145:6 who
made sky and land,
sea and all that *is* in them –
145:7 who
guards truth in *the* age.
He works judgment
for those suffering injury.
He gives food to *the* hungry.
He frees *the* shackled.

145:8 God
gives *the* blind light.

God raises *the* crushed.
God delights in *the* fair.
145:9 *The* Lord
guards strangers.
He will support orphan
and widow,
and will *the* ruin sinners' way.
145:10 *The* Lord
will reign in *the* ages –
Your God, Sion,
in generation after generation.

Psalm 146:1 (KJV Ps 147)
Alleluia.
Of Haggai and Zechariah.

Praise *the* Lord,
because *He is* good!
May *a* psalm to our God
be pleasing, beautiful,
and worshipful.
146:2 Building Jerusalem,
the Lord will gather
Israel's scattered *ones* –
146:3 *God,* who heals
the contrite in heart,
and binds up their griefs;
146:4 who numbers
the stars' multitude,
calling all of them by name.

146:5 Our Lord *is* great,
and His strength is great.
There is no number
to His wisdom.
146:6 *The* Lord *is*
sustaining *the* humble,
but bringing sinners down
even to *the* ground.
146:7 Hold fast
to *the* Lord in confession!

Sing psalms to our God
on guitar –
146:8 who
covers sky with clouds,
and prepares rain for *the* land;
who produces grass

in *the* mountains,
and herbs for men's slaves!
146:9 He gives
food to His cattle
and to *the* crows' chicks,
invoking Him.

146:10 He
will not have pleasure
in *the* horse's strength,
nor will man's legs
be pleasing to Him.
146:11 *The* Lord is pleased
over those who fear Him,
and those hoping
in His mercy.

Psalm 147:1[85]
Alleluia.

Praise *the* Lord, Jerusalem!
Praise your God, Sion,
147:2 because He
strengthened your gates' bars!
He blessed your children
in you –
147:3 who established
your borders in peace,
and satisfies you
with *the* grain's fat –
147:4 who sends
out His word to *the* land!
His word runs quickly –
147:5 who
gives snow like wool.

He scatters cloud like ash.
147:6 He sends
His ice like morsels,
before His cold's face.
Who can sustain *it*?
147:7 He sends out His word
and will melt it.
His wind will blow
and waters will flow –
147:8 God, who announces
to Jacob His fairness,
and to Israel His judgment.

---

[85] The beginning of Psalm 147 in the Vulgate corresponds to Psalm 147:12 in the RSV. Thereafter, the Vulgate chapter numbering agrees with the numbering of standard English Bibles.

147:9 He
has not worked this way
with other nations.
His judgment was not
made known to them.

Psalm 148:1
Alleluia.

Praise *the* Lord
from *the* skies!
Praise Him in *the* heights!
148:2 Praise Him,
all His messengers!
Praise Him, all His armies!
148:3 Praise Him,
sun and moon!
Praise Him, all stars and light!
148:4 Praise Him,
sky of skies,
and water which is
above *the* sky!
148:5 Praise
the Lord's name,
because He spoke
and they were made!
He commanded
and they were created.
148:6 He
stood them in *the* age,
and in *the* age of ages.
He placed *a* precept
and will not disregard *it*.

148:7 Praise
the Lord from *the* land,
dragons and all abysses –
148:8 fire, hale, snow, ice,
stormy winds which will do
His word –
148:9 mountains and all hills,
fruit-bearing trees

and all cedars –

148:10 beasts and all cattle,
snakes and feathered birds –
148:11 land's kings
and all peoples,
princes and all
the land's judges –
148:12 young
men and young women,
elders with youth –
let them praise
the Lord's name,
148:13 because His name
alone is exalted!
148:14 His confession
is over sky and land,
and His people's strength
will be lifted up –
a hymn by all His holy ones,
Israel's children,
people drawing close to Him.

Psalm 149:1
Alleluia.

Sing to *the* Lord *a* new song!
Sing His praise
in *the* holy ones' gathering!
149:2 Let Israel be happy
in Him who made him.
Let Sion's children exult
in their King.
149:3 Let them
praise His name in choir.
Let them chant psalms to Him
in tympani and stringed
instrument,
149:4 because *the* Lord
is pleased in His people.
He will lift up *the* gentle
in security.
149:5 Holy ones
will exult in glory.
They will be happy
in their beds.
149:6 God's exaltations
will be in their throats,
and two-edged swords
in their hands,
149:7 to working
revenge among nations,
rebukes among peoples –
149:8 to binding
their kings in fetters,
their nobles in iron cuffs –
149:9 that they may work
the judgment written
against them.

This is glory to all His holy ones.

Psalm 150:1
Alleluia.

Praise *the* Lord
among His holy ones!
Praise Him
in His strength's foundation!
150:2 Praise Him
in His mighty works!
Praise Him according to
the multitude of His
greatness!
150:3 Praise Him
with *the* trumpet's sound!
Praise Him
on stringed instrument
and guitar!
150:4 Praise Him
with tympani and choir!
Praise Him
on strings and organ!
150:5 Praise Him
with well-sounding cymbals!
Praise Him
in jubilations' cymbals!
150:6 Let every breath
praise *the* Lord![86]

---

[86] The Vulgate and Septuagint add a further Psalm, Psalm 151, not found in most English scriptures. It is given here as a footnote.

Psalm 151:1
This psalm was written
by David himself,

and outside *the* number,
when he had fought
with Goliath.
I was small
among my brothers,
and youngest
in my father's house.
I pastured my father's sheep.
151:2 My hands made *an* organ.
My fingers prepared
a stringed instrument.
151:3 Who will announce *it*
to my Lord?
He is *the* Lord.
He will hear all.
151:4 He sent His angel and took
me from my father's sheep,
and anointed me
in His anointing's mercy.
151:5 My brothers were good
and large,
yet *the* Lord's pleasure
was not in them.
151:6 I came out
against *the* foreigner.
He cursed me by His idols.
151:7 But I unsheathed from him
his own sword.
I cut off his head
and took shame away
from Israel's children.

Other Translations by Searchlight Press

In this series:

<u>The Way of Wisdom: Job, Proverbs, Ecclesiastes, Song of Solomon</u> (English and Latin-English editions available. Published September 2008)

<u>The Audacity of Prayer: a Fresh Translation of the Book of Psalms</u> (English and Latin-English editions available. Published April 2009)

<u>Daniel and the Minor Prophets</u> (English and Latin-English editions available. Due October 2009)

Searchlight Press
Who are you looking for?
Publishers of thoughtful Christian
books since 1994.
PO Box 482
Glen Rose, Texas 76042
888.896.6081
info@Searchlight-Press.com
www.Searchlight-Press.com
www.JohnCunyus.com

www.ingramcontent.com/pod-product-compliance
Lightning Source LLC
Chambersburg PA
CBHW060514100426
42743CB00009B/1315